Cracking the Fertile Code: Unveiling the Secrets to Timing Intercourse for Pregnancy

By

Amy J. Wheeler

Disclaimer:
The information provided in this book, "Cracking the Fertile Code: Unveiling the Secrets to Timing Intercourse for Pregnancy," is for educational and informational purposes only. It is not intended to be a substitute for professional medical advice, diagnosis, or treatment. Always seek the advice of your physician or other qualified health provider with any questions you may have regarding a medical condition. Never disregard professional medical advice or delay in seeking it because of something you have read in this book. The author and publisher disclaim any liability whatsoever in connection with the use of this information.

About the Author: Amy J. Wheeler

Amy J. Wheeler is not only a devoted mother but also a seasoned content creator with a wealth of experience in the field of reproductive health. Drawing from her own journey to parenthood and her extensive research in fertility science, Amy offers a unique perspective that resonates with readers worldwide. Her ability to distill complex information into accessible and actionable insights has earned her a reputation as a trusted authority in the field. With a genuine passion for helping others achieve their dreams of starting a family, Amy's writing is both informative and inspiring, reflecting her unwavering commitment to supporting individuals on their path to conception and beyond.

Table of Contents

Introduction:

Cracking the Fertile Code, Unveiling the Secrets of Timing Intercourse for Pregnancy

Many people's emotions are warmed by the desire to become parents, yet getting pregnant isn't always easy. A waltz over flowery meadows, brimming with the delight of imminent expectation, is what it is for some. Some see it as a journey through difficult landscapes that will test their mettle and teach them to trust their body more.

You will find this book, "Cracking the Fertile Code," to be an invaluable resource on this path. Unveiling its mysteries and giving you the power to match your actions with its natural rhythm, we explore the intriguing world of the menstrual cycle. In this book, you will learn how to achieve pregnancy by strategically dancing around the guesswork involved in timing your intercourse.

Put away those one-size-fits-all ovulation kits and strict calendars. We provide you the tools you need to master your menstrual cycle, allowing you to recognize its subtle signals and find your fertile window. Imagine the peace of mind that comes with knowing exactly when to establish the optimum conditions for conception, replacing fear with educated certainty.

But that's not all this book covers. We explore the impact of lifestyle choices on your fertility potential, offering practical recommendations on enhancing your nutrition, exercise, and stress management. We also cover frequent issues couples confront, providing insight and help to handle them effectively.

Whether you're a seasoned cycle tracker or just started on this adventure, "Cracking the Fertile Code" is your roadmap to revealing the mysteries within you. With its straightforward explanations, practical methods, and motivating insights, this book gives you the knowledge and confidence to crack the fertile code and enjoy the miracle of life.

The Importance of Timing Intercourse: Imagine trying to catch a train without knowing its schedule. Your odds of success wouldn't be great, right? The same approach applies to conception. While sperm can survive for a few days and an egg lives for around 24 hours after ovulation, timing intercourse around your fertile window dramatically boosts your chances of conception. Let's go deeper into the "why" behind this:

The Fertile Window: Your Prime Time for Conception

Think of your menstrual cycle as a window with blinds partially open for a short period. This window symbolizes your reproductive window, often covering 5 days: 3 days leading up to ovulation and the day of ovulation itself. Outside this window, the blinds are mostly closed, making conception exceedingly unlikely.

Sperm and Egg: A Time-Sensitive Rendezvous

Sperm can remain around for 3-5 days, waiting for the egg's arrival. However, their quality and motility deteriorate over time. The egg, on the other hand, only lives for roughly 24 hours following ovulation. So, for a successful fertilization, the sperm needs to be present in the fallopian tubes when the egg is released: a time-sensitive rendezvous!

Maximizing Your Chances: Intercourse in the Fertile Window

By having sex during your fertile window, you dramatically improve the odds of sperm encountering the egg within its short existence. This planned timing ensures:

More sperm availability: By having intercourse every other day or daily within your viable window, you ensure a fresh supply of sperm is waiting for the egg, even if ovulation occurs somewhat earlier or later than predicted.

Optimal sperm quality: Since sperm quality degrades with time, having sex closer to ovulation maximizes the odds of fertilization by a healthy, motile sperm.

Reduced stress and anxiety: Knowing you're behaving in tune with your cycle's natural rhythm might ease the stress and anxiety commonly involved with attempting to conceive.

Bear in mind that every woman's cycle is unique, and your fertile window may fluctuate somewhat month to month. By learning to observe your cycle and comprehend its indications, you acquire the power to determine your individual fertile window and time intercourse for optimal conception.

This knowledge, together with the information and resources presented in this book, will empower you to turn your path from a guessing game to a purposeful and informed pursuit of parenthood. Are you ready to unlock the secrets of your cycle and enhance your chances of conception? Dive further into the intriguing world of your menstrual cycle and discover the power of timing intercourse for pregnancy!

While timing intercourse plays a critical role, conception includes more than merely hitting the right time. Think of it like planning a garden for the perfect bloom: building a fertile environment within your body works hand-in-hand with precise timing. In this section, we'll explore:

Lifestyle Choices: Cultivating a Fertile Landscape

Your food, exercise habits, stress levels, and even sleep patterns can all influence your overall reproductive potential. We'll delve into:

Nourishing your body: Discover the critical nutrients and dietary choices that support healthy egg and sperm development, hormone balance, and overall reproductive health.

Moving your body: Explore how regular exercise promotes hormonal balance, enhances blood flow to the reproductive organs, and regulates stress, contributing to a fruitful environment.

Taming the stress monster: Stress wreaks havoc on hormones and ovulation, so we'll arm you with practical suggestions on stress management and relaxation techniques to nurture a calmer, more fertile condition.

Sleep for success: Uncover the link between appropriate sleep and healthy hormone levels, and learn how to prioritize restorative sleep for maximum fertility.

By making informed choices about your lifestyle, you build a fertile oasis within your body, setting the stage for conception success.

Addressing Common Roadblocks: Navigating the Journey

The route to parenthood isn't always smooth sailing. We'll discuss frequent issues couples experience, such as:

Irregular cycles: Learn tactics for tracking and interpreting irregular cycles, and explore alternative approaches for finding your reproductive window.

Low sperm count: Discover lifestyle adjustments and various therapies to encourage healthy sperm production in your partner.

Medical issues: We'll provide help on navigating certain medical disorders that may impair fertility, including information and support choices.

Remember, you're not alone on this path. We'll provide you with the information and resources to confront difficulties effectively and seek expert help when needed.

The Journey Continues:
By understanding your cycle, scheduling intercourse wisely, and boosting your total reproductive potential, you empower yourself to traverse this road with confidence. Note that conception is a difficult dance, and this book is your guide to learning the moves. Join us as we continue to expose the secrets of your cycle and empower you to unlock the fertile code towards realizing your dream of parenting.

Challenges of Timing Intercourse for Pregnancy

While identifying your fertile window and timing intercourse correctly are key steps towards conception, let's be honest: it's not always easy. Life throws curveballs, and handling the mechanics of intimacy around your fertile window can provide unique obstacles.

The Pressure Play: Trying to conceive can heighten the pressure around sex, making what should be a pleasant act into a job. This can lead to performance anxiety and decreased enjoyment, ironically reducing the very act supposed to start life. Remember, communication and openness are crucial. Discuss expectations and worries with your spouse, promoting closeness and enjoyment alongside conception efforts.

Life Doesn't Stop:

Work schedules, social responsibilities, and unexpected events might disturb the most painstakingly planned intercourse time. Don't fall into the trap of rigorous scheduling — remember, your reproductive window is more than simply one day. Remain flexible, prioritize communication, and be spontaneous when feasible.

Charting Fatigue: Tracking your cycle may become boring, especially if you haven't conceived rapidly. Acknowledge the emotional toll and seek help from loved ones or internet forums. Consider streamlining your tracking approach or taking breaks as needed.

Irregular periods: For women with irregular periods, predicting ovulation and the fertile window might feel like playing darts blindfolded. Don't despair! Explore alternate FAMs like cervical mucus observation or consider visiting a healthcare expert for individualized counsel.

Reduced Libido: Stress, weariness, and even drugs can impair your libido, making sex less desirable. Focus on stress management, talk freely with your partner, and try different means of intimacy that don't only focus on conception.

Medical Challenges: Underlying medical issues, such endometriosis or hormone imbalances, might affect your cycle and fertility. Don't hesitate to seek professional help if you feel a medical issue may be limiting your efforts.

Remember:
These challenges are real, but they are not insurmountable. Embrace flexibility, maintain open communication, and prioritize your well-being. your book equips you with knowledge and tools, but remember, you are not alone on your path. Seek support from healthcare experts, internet networks, or trustworthy friends when needed.

By accepting the challenges and approaching them with compassion and kindness, you may transform them into opportunities for growth and connection. So, breathe deeply, embrace the ups and downs, and continue your path towards breaking the fruitful code, hand-in-hand with information and assistance.

While "Cracking the Fertile Code" focuses on the science and tactics of increasing your odds of conception, remember that this journey is deeply personal and emotional. This section addresses the emotional terrain around attempting to conceive, offering support and assistance as you traverse this sometimes-challenging yet ultimately hopeful route.

The Emotional Rollercoaster: The experience of trying to conceive can be fraught with emotions such as hope, enthusiasm, frustration, disappointment, and all in between. For your own wellbeing and the success of your journey, it is imperative that you acknowledge and deal with these feelings.

Controlling Anticipations: Remember that conception doesn't always happen right away and set reasonable expectations. Acknowledge little triumphs along the way and refrain from evaluating your path against that of others.

Acknowledging Disappointment: It's common to experience disappointment when conception takes longer than anticipated. Remind yourself that you're not alone when you chat to others who will support you and give yourself time to work through these feelings.

Speaking with Your Spouse: It's critical to communicate honestly and openly with your partner. Establish a secure environment where each other may express themselves by sharing your worries, thoughts, and hopes.

Seeking Support: Encircle yourself with encouraging family and friends, think about getting involved in internet forums, or get professional assistance from a therapist or counselor. This is not a journey you have to go alone.

Sustaining Closeness Beyond Conception: Keep in mind that having sex shouldn't be limited to being pregnant. During the procedure, give your partner's physical and emotional closeness first priority. Investigate different kinds of intimacy, concentrate on creating a safe and loving relationship, and keep in mind that the journey is a crucial component of the narrative.

Celebrating Your Body: Give your body due respect and gratitude for its amazing capacity to bear life. Take care of yourself, partake in enjoyable activities, and cultivate your general wellbeing.

Recall that being pregnant is an extremely personal experience with its own set of difficulties and successes. You'll be more equipped to handle this period with poise, resiliency, and hope if you embrace the emotional journey in addition to the scientific understanding. Although this book provides assistance and direction, never forget that you are the writer of your own tale. Accept its complexities, acknowledge your fortitude, and never lose sight of the goal that inspires you on your path.

Understanding your menstrual cycle and strategically timing sexual activity will increase your chances of becoming pregnant. "Cracking the Fertile Code" will provide you with the knowledge and skills to do this. It gives you the ability to go past a "guessing game" mentality and adopt a path that involves proactive action and well-informed decision-making.

This is an overview of what you will discover:

Demystifying your cycle:
Recognize the various stages of your menstrual cycle and how they affect your ability to conceive.

To determine your viable window, learn to read important physiological cues such as basal body temperature and cervical mucus.

Choose the fertility awareness methods (FAM) that best fits your needs and way of life by investigating the different options available.

Increasing your chances:
Learn how important it is to have sex during your reproductive window in order to conceive at your best.

Recognize the effects that lifestyle decisions like nutrition, exercise, stress relief, and sleep quality can have on your ability to conceive.

Discover how to deal with typical problems like irregular periods, poor sperm counts, and illnesses.

Getting over the emotional terrain:
Examine the spectrum of feelings related to attempting to become pregnant and create constructive coping strategies.

Acquire skills in handling expectations, having productive conversations with your spouse, and asking for help from family or experts when needed.

Along the way, learn how to cultivate intimacy and self-care.

This book does more than just impart knowledge. It promotes a comprehensive strategy for conception, taking into account both the practical and emotional components of this process. "Cracking the Fertile Code" makes it possible for you to take an active role in your own fertility journey by providing you with clear explanations, useful tools, and motivating insights. This will increase your chances of success and help you develop a positive and empowering mindset as you go.

So let's get started on this exciting journey together. Turn the page to reveal the mysteries that lie ahead!

Chapter One:

Understanding Your Cycle

Your menstrual cycle could seem like a convoluted riddle, leaving you feeling like you're flying blind on your route to parenthood. But fear not! In this chapter, we'll go on a journey of unraveling your cycle's secrets, transforming it from a complex jigsaw into a clear blueprint to enhance your fertility.

We'll delve into the fundamentals of your cycle, investigating the complicated dance of hormones and the interesting responsibilities of each phase. You'll develop a detailed grasp of how ovulation plays a critical part in conception, and how each phase lays the framework for a prospective pregnancy.

Forget convoluted terms and intricate charts. We'll break down the science into easily accessible information, helping you to become an expert on your own unique cycle. Imagine the sense of firmly identifying the cues your body sends, forecasting your viable window with ease, and finally knowing the rhythm that drives your reproductive health.

So, let's enter into this empowering exploration together. By the end of this chapter, you'll be well on your way to cracking the code of your cycle, uncovering the secrets to optimize your chances of conception and embrace your journey with fresh knowledge and confidence.

Now that we've kindled the spark of interest, let's explore deeper into the delicate symphony of your menstrual cycle. Each phase, like a different movement, plays a critical function in the grand finale of ovulation and eventual pregnancy.

1. The Follicular Phase: Blossoming Potential
Imagine this as the opening act, where your body prepares the stage for a future pregnancy. Hormones like estrogen surge, promoting the creation of follicles in your ovaries, each holding a valuable egg. This phase sets the tone for the rest of the cycle, and its length might vary from woman to woman.

2. Ovulation: The Spotlight Moment
This is the culmination of the cycle, where the star of the show – the egg – takes center stage. A surge in hormones promotes the release of a mature egg from one of your ovaries, ready to meet its potential spouse. This period is normally

short, lasting approximately 24 hours, but understanding its timing is critical for optimizing your chances of conception.

3. The Luteal Phase: Anticipation and Transformation
After ovulation, the empty follicle turns into a corpus luteum, producing progesterone, a hormone crucial for preparing the lining of your uterus for a prospective pregnancy. This phase is filled with anticipation, as your body waits to see if fertilization occurs. If it doesn't, progesterone levels decrease, leading to menstruation and the start of a new cycle.

4. Menstruation: Renewal and Reset
This phase signals the conclusion of the current cycle and the beginning of a new one. The lining of your uterus, no longer essential for pregnancy, sheds as menstrual flow. It's a striking reminder of your body's natural rhythm and its ability to rejuvenate itself each month.

Each woman's cycle is unique, and the length of each phase might vary. However, understanding the basic tasks of each phase helps you to connect the dots and read your body's messages with better clarity.

1. The Basics of the Menstrual Cycle

While understanding the four phases of the menstrual cycle is vital, a fully thorough grasp involves delving deeper into the twisted distinctions and their impact on conception. So, let's shed the basic framework and highlight the complex workings of your cycle:

Phase 1: The Follicular Phase (Menstruation to Ovulation)

The menstrual cycle's opening act, the Follicular Phase, may seem like a peaceful transition, yet beneath the surface, a vibrant drama unfolds. Let's go deeper into this essential phase, investigating its intricacies and their impact on your reproductive journey:

Menstruation: The Curtain Rises

Shedding the Past: This 3-7 day phase isn't only about blood loss; it's the shedding of the previous cycle's endometrial lining, a preparation for a potential fresh beginning. Think of it like cleaning the stage for a fresh performance.

Hormonal Shifts: Estrogen levels are low, while FSH (follicle-stimulating hormone) takes center stage. FSH acts like a conductor, encouraging the growth of many follicles (small sacs) in your ovaries, each holding an immature egg.

Follicular Selection: It's a competition within the ovaries! While numerous follicles continue to expand, only one will be chosen to become dominant and release an egg during ovulation. This selection process is highly impacted by increased estrogen levels produced by the developing follicles.

Estrogen: The Stage Designer

Building the Nest: Estrogen performs a critical function in preparing the uterus for a prospective pregnancy. It encourages the thickness of the endometrium, converting it from a thin layer to a plush, nutrient-rich lining, ready to welcome an embryo. Imagine it as making a snug nest for a lovely egg.

Mucus Matters: Estrogen also changes cervical mucus, making it more slippery and clear around ovulation. This "fertile mucus" creates a suitable environment for sperm to migrate and contact the egg. Think of it as a welcoming road for the potential father.

Signs and Symptoms: While modest, your body may transmit indications during this phase. You might notice greater energy levels, cleaner skin, and a heightened libido, all attributable to elevated estrogen.

Tracking Fertility Signs: Becoming Your Own Detective

The Follicular Phase offers modest signals regarding your reproductive window. By being a detective of your own body, you can unlock these crucial clues:

Cervical Mucus: Pay attention to changes in its consistency and texture. Around ovulation, it becomes more slippery and transparent, like egg white - a sign of peak fertility.

Basal Body Temperature (BBT): This involves taking your temperature first thing in the morning before any activity. After ovulation, progesterone induces a modest rise in BBT, creating a biphasic pattern on a chart. While not infallible, BBT can assist confirm ovulation has happened.

Other Indicators: Some women experience mittelschmerz (mid-cycle pain) or ovulation spotting around ovulation, presenting further hints to their reproductive window.

Note:
Individuality Matters: The Follicular Phase can vary in length amongst women, ranging from 7 to 21 days. Observing your own cycle patterns throughout time is crucial to knowing your particular rhythm.

Holistic Approach: While ovulation is critical, the Follicular Phase plays a vital function in preparing your body for conception. Optimizing your health and lifestyle during this phase can add to total reproductive potential.

Embrace the Journey:
The Follicular Phase may seem peaceful, but it's a key act laying the stage for the drama to emerge. By learning its nuances and observing your body's signals, you become an active participant in your reproductive journey, empowered to make informed choices towards realizing your desire.

So, don't underestimate the potency of the Follicular Phase. By enjoying its subtle dance, you get crucial insights into your body and unlock the secrets to enhancing your fertility potential, paving the way for a more informed and empowering journey towards conception.

Phase 2: Ovulation - The Spotlight Moment of Your Cycle

Imagine the curtains rising, the orchestra playing, and all eyes on the stage. In your menstrual cycle, ovulation is the dramatic highlight, the moment the star of the show — the mature egg – takes center stage, ready for its chance to meet its spouse. Let's discuss this key period in detail:

The LH Surge: The Grand Finale
This is the essential event that induces ovulation. As the dominant follicle matures in the previous phase, it produces increasing levels of estrogen. This growing estrogen level sends a signal to your pituitary gland, urging it to generate a surge of luteinizing hormone (LH). Think of it as the conductor raising their baton, cueing the big finale.

The Egg's Release: Stepping into the Spotlight
The LH surge causes a chain reaction within the dominant follicle. Its wall weakens, and the

mature egg breaks forth, signaling ovulation. This normally happens around day 14 of a 28-day period, but remember, cycles can vary. The discharged egg has a lifespan of around 24 hours, waiting patiently in the fallopian tube for a prospective contact with sperm.

Identifying Ovulation: Becoming Your Own Detective
While you can't immediately feel ovulation happening, your body provides subtle clues:

Mittelschmerz: Some women have minor pain or cramping around ovulation, usually on one side of the lower abdomen. This discomfort denotes the follicle rupturing and releasing the egg.

Ovulation Spotting: Light spotting owing to hormonal fluctuations might occur around ovulation. It's vital to separate this from usual menstrual bleeding.

Cervical Mucus: As discussed previously, fertile-quality cervical mucus becomes clear, elastic, and egg-white-like around ovulation, producing a receptive environment for sperm.

Basal Body Temperature (BBT): After ovulation, progesterone levels rise, creating a slight but consistent increase in BBT. Tracking your BBT chart can confirm ovulation has occurred, but keep in mind it doesn't forecast ovulation itself.

Ovulation Predictor Kits (OPKs): These kits detect the LH surge in your urine, signaling that ovulation is about to happen. However, they don't pinpoint the exact moment, therefore other approaches are necessary for confirmation.

Optimizing Your Chances:
Understanding your fertile window, the 5 days around ovulation (including ovulation day itself), is vital for maximizing your chances of conceiving. By observing your body's symptoms and utilizing tools like BBT charting or OPKs, you may identify this window and deliberately time intercourse for best results.

Note:
Individuality Matters: Not everyone experiences all these signs, and the intensity can vary. Observe your own body's unique rhythms and uncover the strategies that work best for you.

Beyond Ovulation: While ovulation is vital, remember that other factors like sperm quality and timing also play a role.

Embrace the Drama:
This is the key phase in your cycle, where the probability of conception arises. By knowing ovulation and your fertile window, you become an active participant in your journey, empowered to make educated choices and embrace the drama of producing life.

So, don't underestimate the relevance of Phase 2. By being a keen watcher of your body's signals and adopting numerous approaches, you may demystify ovulation and traverse this vital window with confidence, moving a significant step closer to attaining your dream of parenting.

Phase 3: The Luteal Phase - Anticipation and Transformation

The spotlight dims in Phase 3, but the drama continues behind the scenes. This "Luteal Phase" is a time of expectation and metamorphosis, where your body prepares for a prospective pregnancy or readies for the next cycle. Let's go more into this important stage:

Progesterone: The Stage Manager
After ovulation, the empty follicle converts into the corpus luteum, a transitory structure pumping out progesterone. This hormone serves a key role in preparing the stage for a potential visitor – the fertilized egg. Progesterone performs its magic in two major ways:

Building the Royal room: Imagine the endometrium as a magnificent room for the embryo. Progesterone increases blood vessel formation and thickens the lining, creating a nutrient-rich environment ideal for implantation. Think of it as preparing a comfortable, welcoming space for the advent of royalty.

Holding Your Breath: Progesterone also suppresses ovulation, limiting the release of another egg and ensuring only one potential pregnancy advances at a time. It's like holding your breath, waiting for the current drama to unfold before commencing a new act.

The Waiting Game: Will There Be an Encore?
If fertilization happens, the embryo travels down the fallopian tube and implants in the thicker endometrium about day 6-10 after ovulation. If implantation happens, the corpus luteum

continues generating progesterone, supporting the early stages of pregnancy.

However, if fertilization doesn't occur, the corpus luteum starts to shrink, and progesterone levels gradually drop. This decline triggers the shedding of the built-up endometrial lining, leading to menstruation and the start of a new cycle. Think of it as the curtain falling on the present act, but with the promise of a fresh performance to come.

Premenstrual Syndrome (PMS): The Understudy Takes the Stage

The hormonal variations during the Luteal Phase, particularly the drop of progesterone, can induce a range of physical and emotional symptoms known as PMS. These can include:

Physical: Bloating, headaches, breast pain, acne

Emotional: Mood swings, impatience, anxiety, exhaustion

Understanding these changes and their triggers might help you manage PMS efficiently. Some strategies include:

Lifestyle modifications: Regular exercise, proper nutrition, stress management, and sufficient sleep can all contribute to relieving PMS symptoms.

Supplements: Consult your doctor about potential benefits of vitamin B6, magnesium, or evening primrose oil.

Over-the-counter medications: Pain medicines like ibuprofen can help control cramping and headaches.

Remember:
Individuality Matters: The intensity and length of PMS symptoms varies widely between women. Observe your personal tendencies and learn what works best for managing your discomfort.

Beyond the Physical: PMS can also influence your mental well-being. Be nice to yourself, exercise self-care, and seek support if needed.

Embrace the Transformation:
The Luteal Phase, despite its obstacles, is a vital part of your cycle. By understanding its purpose and managing PMS well, you may navigate this phase with better ease and appreciation for its role in your overall reproductive health.

So, don't underestimate the relevance of Phase 3. While it may feel less dramatic than ovulation, it's a key period of preparation, anticipation, and ultimately, transformation.

By accepting this phase and its particular challenges, you get a deeper awareness of your body and empower yourself to navigate your reproductive journey with educated decisions and a balanced viewpoint.

Phase 4: Menstruation - Renewal and Reset, Not Just an Ending

Menstruation, frequently perceived as the "ending" of your cycle, is more correctly considered as a dramatic rebirth and reset, clearing the way for a fresh potential pregnancy journey. Let's investigate this final phase in detail, appreciating its physical, emotional, and overall significance:

Lining's Farewell: A Release and Rejuvenation With no pregnancy in the Luteal Phase, progesterone levels fall. This dip marks the loss of the thicker uterine lining, leading to menstrual flow. This process, spanning 3-7 days with an average blood loss of 30-40ml, isn't only about expelling waste. Think of it as a strategic release, clearing the stage and preparing the ground for a fresh start.

Cycle Variations: Embracing Your Uniqueness
While a 28-day cycle is typically discussed, understand that regular cycles can range from 21 to 35 days. Understanding your own unique cycle pattern, including its length and changes, is vital for precisely determining your fertile window and optimizing your chances of conception. Track your cycle consistently to understand its rhythm and potential deviations.

Beyond Physical Changes: Recognizing the Emotional Landscape
Menstruation doesn't simply impact your body; it can also influence your mood, energy levels, and sleep. Fluctuating hormones can sometimes produce premenstrual syndrome (PMS) with symptoms like cramps, bloating, irritability, and fatigue. Additionally, individuals suffer emotional swings including melancholy, anxiety, or heightened sensitivity.

Embracing Emotional Fluctuations:
Acknowledge that these shifts are normal and part of your cyclical nature. Don't judge yourself;

instead, exercise self-care and kindness.
Prioritize activities that nurture your well-being,
such as light exercise, relaxation techniques,
good food, and connecting with loved ones.
Remember, understanding these cyclical
emotional shifts helps you to manage them
successfully and keep a balanced overall
well-being.

Holistic View: Menstruation and Your Overall
Health
Menstruation offers vital insights into your
general reproductive health. Regular, predictable
cycles often suggest hormonal balance and a
healthy reproductive system. Conversely,
irregular cycles or severe bleeding could require
evaluation by a healthcare practitioner.

Remember:
Menstruation is an important aspect of your
menstrual cycle, not just an ending. It implies
rejuvenation, resets the stage for prospective
conception, and provides crucial health
information.

Embrace the originality of your cycle. Track your
patterns and discover your individual rhythm.

Acknowledge and manage emotional changes. Self-care routines and understanding are crucial to handling this portion of your cycle.

View menstruation holistically. It's a window into your overall reproductive health and can direct you towards informed decisions.

By understanding menstruation beyond its physical characteristics and recognizing its multidimensional nature, you may transform your relationship with this critical season.

Embrace it as a powerful sign of your body's natural cycle, a moment for self-care, and a chance to acquire essential information for optimizing your overall health and fertility journey.

Holistic Approach: Fertility isn't only about ovulation; understanding each phase and their interplay empowers educated decision-making.

By understanding the delicate dance of your menstrual cycle, you access a treasure trove of knowledge about your body and fertility. This helps you to navigate conception with confidence, making informed choices and increasing your chances of attaining your dream of parenthood.

2. Tracking Your Menstrual Journey

Understanding your menstrual cycle is much more than just predicting your period. It's about empowering yourself with information about your body and its natural cycles. Tracking your cycle can yield vital insights into your overall health, fertility, and well-being. In this chapter, we'll look into the numerous ways to track your cycle and analyze the benefits of doing so.

Why Track Your Cycle?
Tracking your cycle has various benefits:

Predicting your period: Knowing when your next period is likely to arrive helps you stay prepared and avoid surprises.

Identifying irregularities: Tracking can help you discover any variations in your cycle's length, duration, or flow, which could signal potential health concerns.

Boosting fertility awareness: Understanding your reproductive window can be important if you're attempting to conceive or avoid pregnancy naturally.

Monitoring PMS symptoms: Tracking can help you notice and manage symptoms like cramps, mood changes, or fatigue linked with premenstrual syndrome (PMS).

Gaining insights into your entire health: Cycle anomalies can occasionally be linked to other health concerns, thus tracking can provide significant information for discussions with your healthcare physician.

Methods for Tracking Your Cycle:

1. Traditional Methods:

A. The Calendar Method: Simplicity with Limitations
Mark the first day of your period on a calendar and calculate the days until your next period. This is a simple procedure, although it may not be as accurate for irregular cycles.

The calendar approach is undoubtedly the simplest way to track your menstrual cycle. It needs no effort, only marking the first day of your period on a calendar and tracking the days until your next one.

However, simplicity comes with limits, especially for irregular cycles. Let's go deeper into the intricacies of this method:

Pros:
Simplicity: No additional tools or apps needed.

Accessibility: Everyone has a calendar, making it readily available.

Discretion: No personal information exchanged with other parties.

Cons:
Accuracy: Only works well for regular cycles (within 7-10 day fluctuations).

Limited Insights: Doesn't capture specifics like flow intensity, symptoms, or ovulation.

Retrospective Tracking: Only tracks past cycles, not forecasting future ones.

Addressing Irregularities:
While the calendar technique might not be perfect for irregular cycles, there are ways to make it more informative:

Track for several months: Record your cycle length for at least 6 months to define a likely range.

Calculate your shortest and longest cycles: Use them to estimate your fertile window (about 14 days before your shortest cycle and ending 1 day before your longest).

Mark the fruitful window with caution: Consider this a "caution zone" where unprotected intercourse might lead to pregnancy.

Note:
The calendar technique is not a dependable means of birth control.
If you have irregular cycles, consider combining it with additional treatments like ovulation tracking or barrier measures.
Consult your healthcare physician for individualized information on tracking and controlling your menstrual period.

B. The Diary Method: Unveiling the Nuances of Your Cycle
Keep a daily diary of your period dates, flow intensity, and any symptoms you have. This method delivers more detail but demands more effort.

The journal approach takes tracking to a more complete level. By keeping a daily journal of period dates, flow intensity, and observed symptoms, you obtain a deeper awareness of your specific cycle's complexity. While requiring more effort than the calendar technique, the detailed information gained holds enormous worth.

Let's discuss its merits, limits, and some tips to make it work for you.

Pros:
Detailed insights: Captures significant information beyond only period dates, providing a comprehensive perspective of your cycle.

Symptom tracking: Helps detect patterns and potential triggers for PMS symptoms, leading to better management options.

Flexibility: Offers complete adaptability in terms of what you track and how, allowing you to personalize your experience.

Historical record: Creates a timeline of your cycle history, enabling you to track changes over time and detect potential trends.

Cons:
Time commitment: Requires daily logging, which may not be possible for everyone.

Data management: Sorting through records and detecting patterns can be tough, especially with long-term tracking.

Subjectivity: Flow intensity and symptom reports can be subjective, thereby influencing data analysis.

Privacy concerns: Sharing your log with others takes careful thinking.

Tips for Effective Diary Tracking:
Use a dedicated notebook or app: Choose a format that encourages consistent logging and facilitates easy data retrieval.

Develop a system: Define categories for documenting dates, flow intensity (e.g., light, medium, heavy), and symptoms (physical, emotional).

Be specific: Use descriptive language for symptoms and note their intensity and duration.

Consider more factors: Track sleep, exercise, stress levels, and other lifestyle factors that can influence your cycle.

Review and analyze: Dedicate time to evaluate your records, detecting trends and probable relationships between symptoms and cycle phases.

Remember:
The journal approach is a great tool, but it's vital to choose a system that works for you and your lifestyle. Consistency and structure are important to reaping its effects.

By embracing the diary technique and incorporating these recommendations, you unleash a treasure mine of self-awareness and empower yourself to navigate your monthly journey with fresh insight and proactive care.

C. Basal Body Temperature (BBT):
Basal Body Temperature (BBT) charting goes further into your cycle's mysteries by studying your daily morning temperature swings. These small adjustments show ovulation, helpful in anticipating your period and understanding your reproductive window.

While requiring attention and potentially altered by external events, BBT charting gives interesting views into your cycle's inner workings.

Pros:
Ovulation confirmation: Identifies ovulation exactly, unlike other procedures, empowering natural family planning or conception efforts.

Proper predictions: With proper charting, you can forecast your period arrival more precisely than other non-temperature-based methods.

Cycle insights: Reveals differences in your cycle length and any underlying health concerns indicated in temperature patterns.

Empowerment: Provides essential knowledge, encouraging a sense of ownership and understanding of your unique cycle.

Cons:
Dedication required: Demands daily temperature measurement at the same moment upon waking, and any disturbances impair accuracy.
Learning curve: Interpreting charts and identifying ovulation can be tough initially, needing attention and experience.

External factors: Sleep problems, illness, or stress might change temperature, potentially influencing chart accuracy.

Not for everyone: May not be realistic for persons with unpredictable sleep cycles or those easily discouraged by potential difficulties.

Tips for Successful BBT Charting:
Invest in a BBT thermometer: Use a sensitive thermometer intended for detecting basal body temperature.

Consistent timing: Take your temperature first thing in the morning, before even getting out of bed, at the same time each day.

Chart effectively: Use a dedicated BBT chart or app to measure your temperature and detect ovulation based on sustained temperature shifts.

Consider external factors: Note down any things like sleep difficulties, illness, or stress that can alter your temperature.

Seek support: Consult online resources, groups, or healthcare specialists for guidance and troubleshooting.

Remember:
BBT charting is a strong tool, but it takes commitment and understanding of its limitations. If you're prepared to invest the effort and are skilled with evaluating data, it can yield significant insights on your cycle's complexity.

Additionally:
Combine BBT charting with other tools like cervical mucus tracking for a more thorough view of your reproductive window.

Consider adopting programs that automate BBT charting and analysis, decreasing the technicalities involved.

Be patient: Consistent tracking over numerous cycles gives more accurate patterns and comprehension of your specific temperature fluctuations.

By embracing BBT charting with the appropriate mindset and technique, you acquire a valuable tool to discover the secrets of your ovulation and empower yourself to manage your fertility or cycle awareness more successfully.
Charting your daily morning temperature can assist pinpoint ovulation and forecast your

period. This strategy needs dedication and can be impacted by variables like sleep disruptions.

D. Cervical Mucus Tracking: Unveiling Fertility's Sticky Secrets

Cervical mucus tracking, commonly dubbed the cervical fluid method, digs into the domain of your body's natural lubricant, offering vital information into your fertile window and general cycle health. By studying the consistency and color of your cervical mucus, you can find crucial information about ovulation and empower yourself to plan accordingly.

Pros:
Cost-effective: Requires no special gear or gadgets, only observation and record-keeping.

Natural and accessible: Works with your body's natural functions, avoiding any external intrusions.

Fertility awareness: Reveals your fertile window with reasonable accuracy, aiding conception or natural birth control approaches.
Cycle knowledge: Provides deeper understanding of your cycle and any hormonal variations.

Cons:
Learning curve: Interpreting variations in consistency and color needs practice and familiarity with your specific cycle.

Subjectivity: Descriptions of mucus features might be subjective, impacting data analysis.

Commitment required: Requires daily observation and documenting, which may not be practical for everyone.

Not foolproof: External factors like arousal or illnesses might change mucus properties, thereby generating misinterpretations.

Tips for Successful Cervical Mucus Tracking:
Observe daily: Check your cervical mucus regularly, either after wiping after using the restroom or by inserting a clean finger into your vagina.

Identify changes: Monitor changes in consistency (sticky, creamy, stretchy) and color (clear, clouded, white).
Track and record: Use a chart or app to log your observations and dates for analysis.

Learn your patterns: Over numerous cycles, find trends in your mucus changes to detect your reproductive window, generally coinciding with stretchy, clear mucus resembling egg whites.

Seek support: Consult online resources, communities, or healthcare professionals for clarity and guidance.

Remember:
Cervical mucus tracking offers significant information, but it's crucial to realize its limitations and subjectivity. Consistent tracking and familiarity with your individual cycle are crucial to maximize its effectiveness.

Additionally:
Combine cervical mucus tracking with additional methods like BBT charting or calendar tracking for a more thorough view of your cycle.

Consider using apps developed for cervical mucus tracking, giving visualizations, educational resources and reminders.

Remember, your comfort level is paramount. Choose a monitoring method that corresponds with your requirements and lifestyle to encourage a good and informative experience.

By embracing cervical mucus monitoring with patience and the appropriate method, you uncover a natural and empowering tool to navigate your cycle and fertility with increased insight and awareness.

2. Digital Tools:

In today's tech-driven world, period tracker applications have transformed menstrual cycle tracking, bringing simplicity, customisation, and a plethora of information at your fingertips. These adaptable tools go beyond simply predicting your period, helping you to delve deeper into your cycle's intricacies and manage your health proactively.

1. Period Tracker Apps:
Numerous free and paid applications offer handy and extensive tracking options. They can anticipate your cycle, ovulation, and reproductive window, document symptoms, and provide instructional resources.

Pros:
Convenience: Track your bike on the go, anytime, anywhere, simply from your smartphone.

Comprehensive features: Many apps offer period, ovulation, and fertile window forecasts, symptom reporting, mood tracking, tailored insights, and educational resources.

Customization: Tailor your experience by picking elements that resonate with your needs and tastes.

Reminders: Set notifications to log your period, symptoms, or medicine use, ensuring you never miss a beat.

Data analysis: Some programs analyze your data over time, discovering potential patterns and providing insights into your general cycle health.

Cons:
Privacy concerns: Be mindful of data privacy policies and use apps with effective security safeguards to secure your sensitive information.

Accuracy limitations: Predictions, especially for ovulation and fertile window, can be less accurate than other older approaches like BBT charting.

Information overload: Some apps could offer excessive information, so choose one that corresponds with your preferred degree of detail.

Subscription costs: Some apps require paid subscriptions for access to premium features.

Popular Period Tracker Apps:

Flo: Offers a holistic approach with period, ovulation, and pregnancy tracking, symptom reporting, tailored insights, and instructional materials.

Clue: Emphasizes data privacy and scientific precision, offering period and ovulation predictions, symptom tracking, and cycle analysis tools.

Period Tracker - Period Calendar: A user-friendly tool with basic tracking functions, period and ovulation forecasts, and a configurable calendar display.

Glow: Combines period tracking with fertility awareness features, delivering individualized insights and educational tools for individuals seeking to conceive.

MyCalendar: Features period and ovulation tracking, symptom journaling, mood tracking, and a community forum for connecting with other users.

Tips for Choosing the Right App:
Identify your needs: What characteristics are most essential to you (e.g., period prediction, symptom tracking, educational resources)?

Consider privacy: Read data privacy policies carefully and choose apps with strong security features.

Start free: Many programs offer free basic capabilities before requiring upgrades. Experiment with a few before committing to a premium subscription.

Read reviews: Check user reviews and ratings to acquire insights into other users' experiences.

Remember:
Period tracker apps are great tools, but they're not alternatives for expert medical advice. If you have questions about your cycle or notice irregular symptoms, consult your healthcare professional.

By embracing the ease and benefits of period tracker apps, you may access a wealth of information about your cycle, empowering yourself to make informed decisions about your health and well-being.

2. Wearable Devices:
Some smartwatches and fitness trackers can measure your cycle based on variations in heart rate, sleep patterns, or skin temperature. However, their accuracy may vary, and they generally lack the specific capabilities of professional period tracker applications.

Wearable Devices: Tracking Your Cycle on the Wrist, But Does it Measure Up?
Smartwatches and fitness trackers have entered the menstruation tracking field, allowing simple wrist-based monitoring of your cycle. However, before jumping in, understanding their strengths and limits is vital to guarantee you're getting the most accurate and informative experience.

Pros:
Passive tracking: No need to manually log data. The device automatically collects vital information throughout the day.

Convenience: Track your cycle seamlessly while going about your regular activity.

Additional health insights: Many devices provide broader health tracking capabilities like sleep monitoring, heart rate variability, and step count, providing a more holistic view.

Discreet: Discreetly monitor your cycle without needing to whip out your phone or log anything manually.

Cons:
Limited accuracy: Cycle predictions based on indirect markers like heart rate or skin temperature can be less precise than specialist approaches like BBT charting or cervical mucus tracking.

Fewer functionality: Many wearable devices lack the detailed features and educational materials given by dedicated period tracker apps.

Data privacy concerns: Consider data privacy regulations carefully, especially if sharing sensitive health information with a fitness tracker firm.

Cost: High-end devices with complex cycle monitoring functions might be pricey.

Popular Wearables for Cycle Tracking:

Fitbit Sense & Versa: Predict periods and fertile windows based on skin temperature variations, offer basic symptom tracking, and provide sleep and stress insights.

Garmin Vivoactive & Lily series: Track menstrual cycles and symptoms, anticipate periods and fertile windows, and offer extra fitness and sleep tracking capabilities.

Apple Watch with iOS 15+: Log period dates, symptoms, and flow intensity, receive period and ovulation predictions, and access educational resources through Health app.

Tips for Using Wearables for Cycle Tracking: Calibrate correctly: Ensure your equipment is calibrated for reliable sleep and heart rate tracking, vital for cycle forecasts.

Combine with other methods: Consider using the wearable alongside a dedicated period tracker app or other tracking methods for more thorough data.

Monitor accuracy: Track your real period dates and compare them to the device's predictions to measure its accuracy for your unique cycle.

Consult a healthcare professional: If you have concerns about your period or encounter irregular symptoms, visit your doctor, regardless of what your wearable gadget advises.

Remember:
Wearable gadgets offer a convenient way to track your cycle, but their accuracy varies, and they may not provide the same degree of detail as specialist period tracker apps.

Choose a gadget with features that correspond with your needs and priorities, and always prioritize expert medical advice as needed.

By understanding the strengths and limits of wearable devices for cycle tracking, you can make an informed decision about whether they offer the best fit for your needs and guarantee you're getting the most relevant insights about your unique cycle.

Chapter Two:

Identifying Your Fertile Window

The fertile window is the time throughout your menstrual cycle when you are most likely to get pregnant. It normally lasts for around six days, commencing five days before ovulation and ending one day following ovulation. Ovulation is the release of an egg from your ovary. Once the egg is released, it can live for roughly 24 hours.

Spermatozoids can survive for up to five days within your body. This indicates that you can get pregnant if you have sex up to five days before you ovulation.The fertile window is distinct for every woman and might fluctuate from month to month.

There are a number of various ways to track your reproductive window, such as utilizing a calendar technique, tracking your cervical mucus, or using ovulation prediction kits.If you are trying to get pregnant, there are a few things you may do to boost your chances of conception. These include having sex regularly during your reproductive window, tracking your ovulation, and avoiding stress.

1. What is The Fertile Window

The fertile window, also known as the ovulatory window, is the 6-day time of your monthly cycle when you're most likely to become pregnant. It begins 5 days before ovulation and finishes 1 day following ovulation.
Here's a breakdown:

Ovulation: Release of an egg from your ovary, which can live for roughly 24 hours.

Sperm lifespan: Sperm can survive for up to 5 days inside your reproductive tract.

These two conditions combined form the fruitful window:

Days 1-4: Less likely to conceive as an egg hasn't matured yet.

Days 5-7: Higher probability of conception as the egg grows and prepares for ovulation.

Day 8 (Ovulation day): Peak window for conception as the egg is liberated and most receptive to sperm.

Day 9: Decreasing possibility of pregnancy as the egg starts degrading.

Days 10-14: Very low possibility of pregnancy as the egg is no longer viable.

Important things to remember:
The fertile window differs for each woman and might even fluctuate from month to month. Factors like stress, illness, and drugs can impact ovulation timing.

No strategy is 100% accurate in pinpointing the fertile window. Even with ideal timing, other things can affect conception.

The fertile window shouldn't be relied upon as a form of birth control. Use reliable techniques like condoms or hormonal contraception for preventing pregnancy.

If you're attempting to conceive or avoid pregnancy, recognizing your reproductive window can be important information.

However, it's vital to discuss your plans with a healthcare practitioner for tailored assistance and dependable contraception alternatives.

Physiology Behind the Fertile Window:

Hormonal fluctuations: The fertile window is managed by a complicated interaction of hormones, notably estrogen and progesterone. As your cycle advances, estrogen levels rise to drive egg development and ovulation. This spike causes the release of luteinizing hormone (LH), which prompts ovulation and ultimately progesterone production. Progesterone prepares the uterine lining for a future pregnancy.

Cervical mucus changes: Throughout your cycle, your cervical mucus changes in consistency and texture, affected by hormonal variations. During your reproductive window, estrogen boosts cervical mucus production, making it thin, transparent, and elastic, resembling egg white. This enhances sperm migration via the cervix towards the fallopian tubes where fertilization can occur.

Basal body temperature (BBT): Your BBT, the lowest body temperature reached during sleep, also displays a modest shift around ovulation. After ovulation, progesterone induces a modest elevation in BBT, which remains elevated until the next menstrual period. Tracking BBT can help pinpoint ovulation and potentially predict the fertile window.

Factors Affecting the Fertile Window:

Cycle regularity: Women with irregular cycles have varied lengths, making it harder to determine the fertile window precisely. However, procedures like OPKs and BBT tracking can still offer useful insights.

Stress: Chronic stress can disrupt hormone homeostasis and change ovulation time, thereby affecting the reproductive window.

Medications: Certain medications, like hormonal birth control or fertility treatments, might impact the menstrual cycle and reproductive window.

Age: As women age, their cycles tend to become more irregular, and the reproductive window may narrow.

Methods to identify the fertile window:

Calendar method: This entails charting your cycle length for several months and calculating ovulation based on a typical 14-day luteal phase (time from ovulation to menstruation). While easy and free, it's less accurate for irregular cycles.

Cervical mucus observation: Observing changes in cervical mucus consistency during your cycle can assist identify fertile days with increased mucus production (egg-white consistency). This strategy demands practice and interpretive abilities.

Basal body temperature (BBT) charting: Daily BBT tracking can reveal a modest temperature increase after ovulation, helping define the post-ovulation phase and potentially estimate the viable window.

Ovulation predictor kits (OPKs): These kits detect the LH spike preceding ovulation, suggesting the fertile window's approach. They're straightforward to use but don't pinpoint ovulation itself and may have occasional false positives or negatives.

Apps and fertility trackers: These incorporate numerous approaches like calendar, BBT, and cervical mucus tracking into a one platform, delivering reminders and insights. However, their accuracy depends on the app and data supplied, and privacy problems arise with some.

Limitations of the fertile window:

Not foolproof: Even during the viable window, other factors including sperm quality and egg health might influence fertilization.

Variability: The fertile window might fluctuate from month to month and is not usually exactly 6 days.

Not a contraceptive method: Relying exclusively on the fertile window to avoid conception is exceedingly unreliable. Use trusted techniques like condoms or hormonal contraception.

Additional considerations:

Consulting a healthcare practitioner: Discussing your cycle and reproductive window with a healthcare professional can provide specific assistance, especially for irregular periods or fertility issues.

Combined approach: Combining procedures like OPKs with BBT or cervical mucus observation can boost accuracy compared to relying on a single method.

Tracking for varied purposes: Whether seeking to conceive or avoid pregnancy, understanding your fertile window can offer significant information. However, the purpose will decide the most suited approaches and interpretations.

Remember, knowing your body's unique signals is vital. Seek professional help for personalized techniques to control your cycle and reproductive window properly.

2. Identifying Your Fertile Window: Unveiling the Different Methods in Detail

The fertile window, that 6-day time when conception is most possible, can be discovered using many approaches, each with its own strengths and limits. Here's a full breakdown of popular methods:

1. Calendar Method:
How it works: Track the beginning day of your cycle for at least 6 months. Subtract 18 from the shortest cycle length and 11 from the longest to estimate your fertile window (days in between). Remember, this is simply an estimate and may not be correct for irregular cycles.

Strengths:
Simplicity: The calendar approach is definitely the easiest and most accessible way to determine your reproductive window. You don't need any special tools or equipment, only a calendar and the ability to chart your periods.

Freemium: This technique is absolutely free, relying purely on information you naturally track.

Accessibility: Everyone can employ this strategy, regardless of financial means or access to specialized technologies.

Weaknesses:
Limited accuracy: This is the biggest shortcoming of the calendar technique. It relies on the assumption of a 14-day luteal phase (time from ovulation to next period), which is not universal. In actuality, luteal phases might range from 10 to 20 days, considerably reducing the accuracy of the fertile window calculation.

Requires long-term tracking: You need to follow your cycle for at least 6 months, ideally longer, to create a reliable pattern and identify your normal luteal phase length. This can be inconvenient and takes commitment.

Ignores individual variability: The technique doesn't incorporate individual variations in cycle duration, which might fluctuate even in normal cycles owing to numerous circumstances like stress, illness, or medication.

Additional Considerations:
Short cycles: For women with habitually short cycles (less than 27 days), the predicted fertile window based on the calendar technique can be erroneous, potentially missing the actual window altogether.

Long cycles: Similarly, for women with long cycles (more than 35 days), the fertile window estimation could be excessively large, making it less helpful in pinpointing the most fertile days.

Irregular cycles: This method is unreliable for women with irregular cycles as the luteal phase length can vary greatly, making any calculation based on a standard range erroneous.

Overall, the calendar technique can be a starting point for women with regular cycles who are okay with its limits and seek a basic awareness of their reproductive window. However, for additional accuracy and individualized insights, consider combining it with other procedures like

cervical mucus observation, BBT charting, or
OPKs.

2. Cervical Mucus Observation:
How it works: Daily, notice and record the
consistency and volume of cervical mucus.
During ovulation, it becomes transparent, elastic,
and resembles egg white (most fertile). Track
changes during your cycle to discover your
body's tendencies.

Strengths:
Natural and cost-effective: This method
harnesses your body's natural signals, requiring
no additional tools or investment.

Holistic insights: Observing cervical mucus
provides a broader perspective on your hormonal
changes throughout the cycle, revealing more
than just ovulation timing.

Empowers self-awareness: By studying your
individual patterns, you receive essential
knowledge about your reproductive health and
fertility.

Weaknesses:
Learning curve: Initially, evaluating the slight variations in mucus consistency can be perplexing and take practice.

Subjective experience: The impression of mucus properties can differ between individuals, sometimes leading to misinterpretations.

Potential for bias: Unconscious expectations or desire for a specific outcome can influence how you interpret the mucus changes.

Detailed Observation:
Frequency: Daily observation is necessary, ideally around the same time each day to reduce any influences from external sources.

Location: Observe the mucous at the vaginal opening, either directly or on toilet paper.

Consistency: Track variations in consistency from sticky/creamy (non-viable) to clear, stretchy, and egg-white-like (most fertile) and back to dry/sticky following ovulation.

Amount: Note the amount of mucus, which also increases on fertile days.

Color: While normally clear or white, minor fading can occur. Foul scents could suggest infection and need medical treatment.

Tips for Success:
Maintain consistent observation: Stick to a daily routine and avoid relying on recollection.

Chart your observations: Record the consistency, amount, and color of mucus everyday.

Learn from patterns: Over time, you'll recognize your own patterns and fertile mucus qualities.

Consult reputable resources: Seek information from trustworthy sources like medical websites or healthcare providers.

Don't be discouraged: Initially, it could be puzzling, but experience and patience will help you decipher the signs.

Remember:
Cervical mucus monitoring is an important tool, but not perfect. Combine it with other ways for enhanced accuracy.

Individual variances abound, therefore recognizing your own patterns is crucial.

If you have prolonged disorientation, discomfort, or unexpected discharge, visit a healthcare expert.

By going deeper into cervical mucus observation, you can reveal vital clues concerning your viable window and overall reproductive health. Embrace the learning process and cherish your body's unique communication mechanism!

3. Basal Body Temperature (BBT) Charting:
How it works: Use a specific thermometer to measure your BBT first thing in the morning before any activities. Chart your temperature regularly and detect a tiny rise (0.4-1°C) after ovulation, marking the end of your reproductive window.

Strengths:
High accuracy potential: When done methodically, BBT charting can be highly precise in detecting ovulation and fertile window, bringing significant insights into your cycle.

Multifaceted: BBT not only signals ovulation but also reflects overall hormonal alterations throughout your cycle, providing a comprehensive picture of your reproductive health.

Empowerment via knowledge: By deciphering your BBT chart, you obtain a deeper awareness of your body's natural cycle and fertility.

Weaknesses:
Commitment and discipline: Daily pre-dawn temperature observations need dedication and can disrupt sleep patterns if not well-integrated into your routine.

Interpretation complexities: Deciphering the BBT chart involves an understanding of tiny temperature variations and other influences that can influence readings.

Not foolproof: While accurate, BBT charting isn't flawless and should be supplemented with other approaches for optimal results.

Detailed Procedure:
Thermometer: Use a basal body thermometer with high sensitivity for exact readings.

Measurement timing: Take your temperature shortly upon waking, before any activity (even getting out of bed) as body temperature naturally increases during the day.

Recording: Log your temperature consistently each morning at the same time, preferably within a 30-minute frame.

Charting: Use a designated BBT chart or a fertility monitoring app to record your temperature daily and visualize the pattern.

Interpretation:
Baseline temperature: Identify your average pre-ovulation temperature, usually lower and consistent.

Post-ovulation shift: After ovulation, progesterone induces a modest (0.4-1°C) spike in BBT that remains elevated until your next period.

External variables: Be aware of circumstances like illness, sleep interruptions, or alcohol usage that can alter your BBT and interpret accordingly.

Tips for Success:
Consistency is key: Maintain rigorous adherence to daily measurements and recording at the same time.

Minimize disruptions: Ensure a pleasant sleep environment and promote a consistent morning routine for temperature assessment.

Seek guidance: Consult a healthcare expert or trusted resources to understand BBT chart interpretation successfully.

Combine methods: For greater accuracy, consider utilizing BBT in conjunction with cervical mucus observation or ovulation prediction kits.

Remember:
BBT charting is a personal journey, and first problems are usual. Be patient and diligent in learning to comprehend your specific chart.

BBT variations might occur due to external events, therefore consider the wider picture while interpreting your chart.

If you face difficulties or uncertainties, don't hesitate to seek professional help from a healthcare specialist.

By embracing the intricacies of BBT charting and integrating it with other methods, you can discover vital insights into your fertile window and empower yourself with knowledge about your reproductive health.

4. Ovulation Predictor Kits (OPKs):
How it works: Use OPKs according to the package instructions, checking pee for a few days before estimated ovulation. A good result (color change) signifies the LH surge and suggests ovulation within 24-48 hours, signifying the start of your fertile window.

Strengths:
Ease of use: OPKs are user-friendly and take minimum effort compared to other approaches like BBT charting.

Rapid findings: You get rapid results within minutes, delivering valuable insights into your impending fertile window.

Convenient access: OPKs are routinely available at drugstores and online, making them conveniently accessible.

Weaknesses:
Cost: Purchasing OPKs adds a price compared to free alternatives like cervical mucus monitoring or calendar methods.

Limited pinpointing: While revealing the LH surge, OPKs don't specify the exact day of ovulation, providing a window of uncertainty.

False positives/negatives: Like any test, OPKs can occasionally yield erroneous findings owing to different circumstances.

Detailed Procedure:
Identify fertile window: Use a calendar app or past cycle data to estimate your next ovulation day.

Start testing: Begin using OPKs a few days before your estimated ovulation, following the particular directions on the kit.

Test frequency: Depending on the kit, you may test once or twice everyday within the anticipated fertile window.

Interpret results: Look for a color shift on the test strip, signifying a positive result and likely LH surge.

Remember:
Positive ≠ ovulation: An LH surge signals ovulation is approaching, however ovulation itself can occur within 24-48 hours after the surge.

Timing matters: Start testing at least 3-5 days before projected ovulation to catch the LH surge's peak.

Not foolproof: False positives can arise owing to drugs or hormonal variations. False negatives are also possible if you test too early or late.

Individual variations: Like other treatments, OPKs could require personal changes based on your cycle length and hormonal trends.

Additional Tips:
Combine methods: For greater accuracy, utilize OPKs in conjunction with BBT charting or cervical mucus observation.

Consider cycle irregularities: OPKs might be less reliable for irregular cycles due to unpredictable LH surges.

Consult a healthcare professional: If you have questions about interpreting results or irregular cycles, seek help from a doctor or other healthcare expert.

By knowing the complexities of OPKs and their limits, you can harness them effectively to acquire vital insights about your fertile window and make informed decisions regarding your reproductive health.

5. Apps and Fertility Trackers:
How it works: Download an app like Flo or Clue, log your cycle data, including period dates, cervical mucus, and BBT (optional). Based on the data, the app estimates your reproductive window and ovulation.

Strengths:
Convenience: These apps condense numerous procedures including calendar tracking, cervical mucus observation, BBT charting, and even OPK integration into one platform.

Reminders and insights: Many apps offer helpful reminders for data entry and personalized insights based on your tracked information.

Accessibility: Readily available on smartphones, they enable easy access to fertility information and tracking tools.

Weaknesses:
Accuracy variability: The accuracy of insights depends significantly on the unique app's algorithms and the quality and consistency of your data input.

Data privacy problems: Some apps raise concerns regarding data collecting and potential sharing methods, necessitating cautious review before trusting your information.

Reliance on self-reporting: The accuracy ultimately rests on your accurate and consistent data entry, demanding commitment and attention to detail.

Choosing the Right App:
Research and compare: Explore several apps, reading reviews and understanding their features, data management procedures, and price strategies.

Prioritize privacy: Opt for apps with transparent data handling policies and strong security measures.

Consider your needs: Choose an app that caters to your specific needs and desired features, whether it's cycle monitoring, ovulation prediction, or educational materials.

Using Apps Effectively:
Be honest and consistent: Accurately track your data everyday and eliminate estimations to ensure informed insights.

Understand limitations: Remember that apps are not perfect substitutes for medical advice or professional supervision.

Seek consultation: If you have concerns or uncertainties, visit a healthcare expert for individualized guidance.

Remember:
Apps can be great tools, but they should not replace your critical thinking and informed decision-making.

Be diligent about preserving your privacy and use apps that prioritize data security.

Consult a healthcare professional for accurate counsel and specific solutions relating to your reproductive health and fertility difficulties.

By combining your knowledge of various approaches, critical evaluation of available apps, and a commitment to personal health awareness, you can traverse the world of fertility tracking efficiently and acquire useful information regarding your individual reproductive cycle.

Note:
No single method is perfect. Combine procedures like OPKs with BBT or cervical mucus monitoring for greater accuracy.

Track your cycle consistently for several months to discover your own patterns and fertile window changes.

Consult a healthcare expert if you have irregular cycles or difficulties determining your reproductive window.

Additional Tips:
Consider things including stress, illness, and drugs that can influence your cycle.

Explore online resources and groups for support and information.

Remember, the fertile window is a window, not a certainty. For reliable contraception, consider trusted methods like condoms or hormonal contraceptives.

By learning these tools and researching what works best for you, you can acquire vital insights about your fertile window and make informed decisions regarding your reproductive health.

3. Tips For Accurately Identifying Your Fertile Window

Here are some thorough tips to assist you precisely pinpoint your fertile window:

Understanding Your Options:

Multiple methods(Combining Strategies for Accuracy): No single method is perfect. Combine different tactics for increased accuracy. Consider these options:

Embarking on a multi-method strategy is the key to uncovering a clearer picture of your fertile window.

Here's a full analysis of each method, its strengths, limits, and how they might be combined for increased accuracy:

1. Calendar Method:

Pros: Simple, free, no further tools needed.

Cons: Less precise, requires charting cycles for at least 6 months, expects a 14-day luteal phase (not true for everyone).

Best for: Women with regular cycles who want a basic grasp.

Combine with: BBT charting or cervical mucus observation for more precise estimations.

Enhance accuracy: Track cycle lengths attentively and alter estimates based on prior patterns.

2. Cervical Mucus Observation:

Pros: Natural, no expense, provides new hormonal insights, promotes self-awareness.

Cons: Requires regular observation and interpretation practice, might be subjective, sensitive to bias.

Best for: Women comfortable with bodily awareness, seeking holistic insights.

Combine with: BBT charting or OPKs for cross-confirmation of fertile window.

Enhance accuracy: Learn your individual mucus patterns over numerous cycles, contact credible resources for interpretation.

3. Basal Body Temperature (BBT) Charting:

Pros: Highly accurate with devotion, indicates hormonal alterations beyond ovulation.

Cons: Requires daily predawn temperature measurements, interpretation challenges, external influences can affect readings.

Best for: Women committed to thorough charting, wanting comprehensive insights into their cycle.

Combine with: Cervical mucus observation or OPKs for further confirmation.

Enhance accuracy: Use a dedicated thermometer, establish constant measurement timing, track sleep patterns for potential temperature effects.

4. Ovulation Predictor Kits (OPKs):

Pros: Easy to use, detects LH rise signaling approaching ovulation.

Cons: Requires purchasing kits, doesn't identify exact ovulation day, can produce false positives/negatives.

Best for: Women who like convenience, want an early sign of approaching ovulation.

Combine with: BBT charting or cervical mucus observation for a larger window comprehension.

Enhance accuracy: Start testing a few days before estimated ovulation, consider individual cycle variances when interpreting results.

5. Apps and Fertility Trackers:

Pros: Convenient, integrate methods in one location, providing reminders and insights.

Cons: Accuracy depends on app quality and data input, requires continuous data inputs, certain apps have privacy risks.

Best for: Tech-savvy women who value convenience and data visualization.

Combine with: Compare data with other methods for cross-verification.

Enhance accuracy: Choose reputable apps with solid privacy policies, prioritize accurate and consistent data entry.

Combining Strategies for Maximum Accuracy: Start with two or three methods: Experiment to determine which combination works best for you.

Track for numerous cycles: Allow time to understand your specific tendencies and refine predictions.

Cross-verify results: Look for agreement between methodologies for higher confidence.

Seek professional guidance: Consult a healthcare practitioner if you have irregular cycles, trouble understanding data, or specific concerns.

Remember:
The fertile window is an estimate, and individual differences exist. While these procedures give significant insights, they are not foolproof for

contraception. Always consult a healthcare expert for reliable assistance on family planning and reproductive health.

By choosing the correct methods, combining them successfully, and remaining alert to your body's specific signals, you may navigate the fertile window with confidence and gather essential knowledge about your reproductive health.

Commitment and Consistency:
Commitment and consistency are key for precisely identifying your fertile window, regardless of the methods you pick. Here are some extra points to highlight:

Tracking Consistency:
Daily is key: Aim for daily data collecting, even if it takes slight alterations to your routine. Consistency ensures you gather all important information and prevent gaps that can alter interpretation.

Same time, every time: For approaches like BBT charting and cervical mucus observation, look for uniformity in timing. This minimizes the impact of external factors like sleep patterns or time of day on your results.

Be truthful: Record precise data based on your observations, avoiding estimates or wishful thinking. Remember, reliable forecasts depend on reliable data.

Tracking for Multiple Cycles:
Patterns over time: Your reproductive window and cycle can change somewhat month to month. Tracking for at least 3-6 cycles helps you to discover patterns, determine your unique range, and refine your forecasts.

Adjusting predictions: As you gather data, use prior trends to adjust your forecasts for future cycles. This helps you anticipate fruitful windows more precisely.

No easy fixes: Understanding your reproductive window takes time and patience. Don't be disheartened if you don't notice immediate results. Stick with it, and you'll progressively get vital insights.

Minimizing Disruptions:
BBT measurement: Invest in a decent quality thermometer and establish a consistent pattern for pre-dawn temperature measurements, especially on weekends.

Minimize distractions and guarantee unbroken sleep for reliable readings.

Cervical mucus observation: Observe mucus features at the same time of day each time, preferably in the morning or before bedtime.

Avoid extraneous elements like lubricants or douches that can change your perceptions.

External factors: Be careful of how things like illness, stress, or drugs can alter your cycle and interpret data properly. Consider tracking these with your observations for a more holistic view.

Bonus Tip:
Use tools and resources to stay motivated and consistent! Track your statistics in apps or charts, set reminders, and join online forums for support and guidance. By keeping devoted and disciplined, you unleash the entire potential of these procedures and empower yourself with knowledge about your reproductive health.

Interpreting and Refining: Tips for Accurately Identifying Your Fertile Window

Identifying your fertile window can be hard, as each method has its own intricacies and possibilities for misinterpretation. Here are some tips to help you deepen your comprehension and get the most accurate picture:

1. Dive Deeper: Understand the Quirks:
Calendar Method: This relies on a predictable cycle, which not everyone has. Track your cycles for several months to determine your personal rhythm.

Cervical Mucus: Learn the varied consistencies and what they mean. Pay attention to changes during your cycle.

Basal Body Temperature (BBT): Understand the small shift in temperature post-ovulation. Charting changes over time will help you recognize your individual trend.

Ovulation Predictor Kits (OPKs): Don't only seek for a positive test, but comprehend the LH spike building up to it.

2. Seek Expert Guidance:
Healthcare professionals: Consult your doctor, gynecologist, or fertility specialist for specific assistance on evaluating your fertility indications and choosing the best treatments for you.

Reliable internet resources: Seek information from credible organizations like Planned Parenthood, ACOG, or NHS websites. Be careful of claims that look too wonderful to be true.

3. Embrace Charting Tools:
Visualize your data: Use clear charts or applications to record and follow your fertility indications. Seeing trends across time might help you notice minor changes and individual variances.

Analyze trends: Don't just record data, analyze it! Look for recurring patterns and how different indications match with your cycle.

Refine your methods: As you get more data and gain understanding, change your tracking strategies to better suit your particular cycle.

Remember:
No method is perfect, and even with meticulous tracking, your fertile window can change somewhat from month to month.
Stress, illness, and other circumstances might influence your cycle. Remain flexible and patient in your tracking trip.

If you have questions or issues interpreting your signs, visit a healthcare expert.

By learning the subtleties, seeking help, and employing charting tools, you may deepen your awareness of your fertile window and make informed decisions about your reproductive health.

Additional Tips:
Here's how they contribute to defining your fertile window more accurately:

1. Consider External Factors:
Acknowledge the impact: This helps explain unexpected differences in your cycle and prevents misinterpretations due to external circumstances.

Make adjustments: If you're nervous or ill, it could be more tough to pinpoint ovulation precisely. Consider this when studying your data.

2. Track Other Variables:
Gain holistic insight: Logging extra elements like sleep, mood, and discharge offers a broader view of your health and cycle changes.

Identify connections: You might identify relationships between these aspects and your fertile window, leading to a more personalized understanding.

3. Embrace Technology:
Simplify tracking: Apps and internet tools can automate data recording, making the process easier and more consistent.

Leverage predictions: Some applications use algorithms to evaluate your data and forecast ovulation, offering further direction.

Access instructional resources: Many applications and websites offer credible information regarding fertility and cycle tracking, boosting your knowledge.

4. Listen to Your Body:
Be mindful: Physical changes like breast tenderness or libido fluctuations can be subtle indicators about your reproductive window.

Combine with other methods: Don't rely only on intuition, but utilize it as a complementing signal with proven tracking systems.

By adding these additional tips, you establish a thorough method to detect your fertile window. Remember, the key is to remain consistent, patient, and adaptable. As you gather more data and gain experience, your understanding of your body and its particular rhythms will become increasingly refined.

Note:
Accuracy is not guaranteed: The fertile window is an estimate, and individual differences exist. Don't rely solely on this information for contraception.

Seek professional guidance: If you have irregular cycles, difficulties understanding results, or concerns about conception or contraception, visit a healthcare practitioner.

By combining these recommendations and researching approaches most suited to your needs, you can attain a more precise grasp of your viable window and navigate your reproductive health path with confidence and knowledge.

Chapter Three:

Irregular Menstrual Cycles and Fertility: Understanding the Impact

1. Irregular Cycles

Having an irregular menstrual cycle, defined as cycles varying more than 35 days or less than 21 days apart, can undoubtedly damage your fertility. Here's a breakdown of common cycle abnormalities and their potential effects:

1. Oligomenorrhea (infrequent periods):
Cause: Occurs when you have fewer than eight periods in a year.

Impact on fertility: Makes determining ovulation more complex. You may have fewer productive days per cycle.

Conceiving tips: Consider recording cervical mucus or using ovulation prediction kits (OPKs) alongside documenting your cycles to identify potential ovulation windows.

Consulting a healthcare practitioner for additional examination and potential treatment options is recommended.

2. Polymenorrhea (frequent periods):
Cause: Occurs when you have more than eight periods in a year, with cycles generally shorter than 21 days.

Impact on fertility: Can make it tougher to discern fertile days from pre-menstrual bleeding. May shorten the luteal phase (time after ovulation when fertilization can occur).

Conceiving tips: Similar to infrequent periods, measuring cervical mucus and OPKs could help detect potential viable windows.

Consulting a doctor to evaluate the underlying reason and discuss treatment options is vital.

3. Amenorrhea (absent periods):
Cause: No periods for three or more consecutive months.

Impact on fertility: No ovulation often occurs, making natural conception problematic.

Conceiving tips: Seek prompt medical attention to diagnose the cause and seek alternative treatment options, including fertility medicines or assisted reproductive technologies (ART) depending on the diagnosis.

4. Anovulatory cycles (cycles without ovulation):
Cause: Periods occur without ovulation, typically with inconsistent timing.

Impact on fertility: No egg release means no prospect of spontaneous pregnancy.

Conceiving tips: Consulting a specialist is necessary to evaluate the underlying cause and discuss alternative treatment options, such as fertility drugs or ovulation induction.

Additional aspects to consider:
Underlying health conditions: Irregular cycles can also be an indication of underlying health concerns including polycystic ovarian syndrome (PCOS) or thyroid disorders. Treating these issues can enhance your cycle regularity and fertility.

Lifestyle habits: Maintaining a healthy weight, reducing stress, and getting regular exercise can all positively affect your menstrual cycle and fertility.

Many circumstances can cause irregular menstrual cycles, ranging from ordinary lifestyle variables to underlying medical disorders.

Here's a breakdown of some likely culprits:

Lifestyle factors:
Lifestyle variables clearly play a substantial impact in affecting menstrual periods and fertility.

Stress:
Impacts on cycle: Chronic stress increases the "fight-or-flight" response, generating stress hormones like cortisol, which can interfere with the delicate hormonal balance essential for ovulation and regular cycles.

Tips for management: Relaxation techniques like yoga, meditation, deep breathing, and spending time in nature can help reduce stress and enhance cycle regularity.

Weight:
Underweight: Low body fat (less than 21%) might decrease estrogen production, perhaps

leading to amenorrhea (missing periods) and impaired fertility.

Overweight: Excess body fat can convert more androgens (male hormones) into estrogen, influencing ovulation and potentially raising the risk of PCOS.

Recommendations: Maintaining a healthy weight within the suggested BMI range (18.5-24.9) will considerably increase cycle regularity and fertility.

Exercise:
Excessive activity: Intense or long-duration exercise (more than 5-6 hours a week) can inhibit ovulation and create irregular periods.

Moderate activity: Regular moderate-intensity exercise (30 minutes most days of the week) helps enhance cycle regularity by controlling hormones and reducing stress.

Key: Finding a good balance between physical activity and rest is vital.

Diet:
Unhealthy eating: Deficiencies in critical minerals including iron, B vitamins, and healthy fats might impact hormone production and ovulation.

Extreme calorie restriction: Very low-calorie diets (less than 1500 calories per day) can disturb hormonal balance and lead to irregular cycles.

Recommendations: Eating a balanced diet rich in fruits, vegetables, whole grains, lean protein, and healthy fats is vital for hormonal health and regular cycles.

Additional factors:
Sleep: Inadequate sleep can disrupt hormone synthesis and decrease cycle regularity. Aim for 7-8 hours of decent sleep per night.

Smoking: Smoking can contribute to irregular periods and early menopause.

Always bear in mind that while lifestyle modifications can greatly affect your cycle, visiting a healthcare professional for specific counsel based on your individual circumstances is always recommended.

They can help you uncover any underlying medical concerns and build a complete plan to control your periods and enhance your fertility.

Medical conditions:
Polycystic Ovary Syndrome (PCOS):
Disrupts hormone balance, leading to irregular ovulation and cycles.

Symptoms: Irregular periods, increased androgen (male hormone) consequences include acne and facial hair, many tiny cysts in ovaries.

Treatment: Lifestyle adjustments (healthy weight, exercise, diet), medicine (birth control tablets to manage hormones, ovulation-inducing medications).

Thyroid disorders: Overactive (hyperthyroidism) or underactive (hypothyroidism) thyroid influences hormone production, influencing ovulation and cycles.

Symptoms: Vary depending on thyroid function, but might include fatigue, weight changes, mood swings, and irregular periods.

Treatment: Medication to modulate thyroid function, frequently lifelong.

Endometriosis: Tissue comparable to the uterine lining grows outside the uterus, producing pain, inflammation, and irregular periods.

Symptoms: Painful periods, pelvic pain between periods, infertility.

Treatment: Hormone therapy, pain management, surgery in severe cases.

Pelvic inflammatory disease (PID): Infection of the reproductive organs, commonly caused by sexually transmitted infections (STIs), can damage tissues and cause irregular cycles.

Symptoms: Pelvic discomfort, abnormal discharge, fever.

Treatment: Antibiotics, potential surgery in extreme cases.

Premature ovarian insufficiency (POI): Early loss in ovarian function, leading to missing periods and probable fertility issues, often before age 40.

Symptoms: Irregular periods, hot flushes, nocturnal sweats, vaginal dryness.

Treatment: Hormone therapy, researching fertility alternatives.

Uterine fibroids: Non-cancerous growths in the uterus can cause heavy bleeding, longer periods, and unpredictable cycles.

Symptoms: Heavy bleeding, pelvic pain, pressure on bladder or bowels.

Treatment: Monitoring, medicines (to decrease fibroids), minimally invasive techniques, surgery in extreme cases.

Cervical polyps: Non-cancerous growths on the cervix, normally generating no symptoms but sometimes leading to irregular bleeding or spotting.

Symptoms: Irregular bleeding, spotting, heavy periods.

Treatment: Removal in most circumstances, usually a straightforward outpatient operation.

Remember, information contained in this book is not a substitute for expert medical advice. If you suffer irregular cycles or suspect any of these problems, visit a healthcare expert for correct diagnosis and treatment. They can examine your unique circumstances, prescribe necessary testing, and discuss the best course of action for your health and fertility.

Other potential causes:

Medications:
Birth control: Some forms, such progestin-only tablets and Depo-Provera, can weaken the uterine lining and sometimes lead to irregular bleeding or spotting. Others, like combined oral contraceptives, can regulate cycles.

Antidepressants and antipsychotics: These can influence hormone levels and potentially cause irregular cycles or missed periods.

Other medications: Blood thinners, steroids, and some chemotherapy treatments can also alter menstrual periods.

Travel with jet lag:
Disrupting your sleep-wake cycle and internal clock can temporarily disrupt your hormone levels and postpone or shorten your cycle.

Tips: Minimize time zone changes where possible, alter your sleep routine gradually, and prioritize light exposure to assist balance your biological clock.

Perimenopause: The years preceding up to menopause (approximately ages 40-55) can induce hormonal abnormalities, leading to irregular cycles, missed periods, and other changes.

Symptoms: Hot flashes, nocturnal sweats, mood swings, vaginal dryness, along with irregular periods.

Management: Lifestyle adjustments including stress management, good food, and exercise can help manage symptoms. Medication or hormone therapy might be essential in some circumstances.

Additional thoughts:
Stressful life events: Divorce, job loss, or other big life upheavals can create temporary cycle anomalies.

Environmental factors: Exposure to some chemicals or poisons might lead to irregular cycles, but more research is needed.

Individual variations: Every woman's biology is different, and their menstrual cycle can be influenced by a unique combination of circumstances.

Remember, this list is not exhaustive, and it's necessary to consult a healthcare expert for a diagnosis and specific guidance. They can do tests, analyze your medical history, and establish the underlying cause of your irregular cycles.

Additionally, while some lifestyle changes can improve general menstrual health, they shouldn't be considered a substitute for medical diagnosis and treatment if an underlying issue is present.

2. Polycystic Ovary Syndrome (PCOS)

Polycystic Ovary Syndrome (PCOS) is a prevalent hormonal imbalance affecting roughly 1 in 10 women of reproductive age. One of its distinguishing traits is irregular menstrual periods, and understanding this relationship can be helpful for managing your health and fertility.

How does PCOS influence cycles?

Hormonal Disruption: PCOS affects the delicate balance of hormones, primarily by raising androgen (male hormone) levels and diminishing insulin sensitivity. This can lead to:

1. Elevated androgens:
Higher levels of androgens, particularly testosterone, can hinder the development of follicles in the ovaries, preventing them from reaching maturity and releasing eggs. This leads to fewer or no ovulations, resulting in irregular or nonexistent periods.

Insulin resistance: PCOS commonly entails insulin resistance, when the body fails to use insulin adequately. This can further disturb hormone balance and contribute to poor ovulation.

Impaired ovulation: Fewer or no mature eggs are produced from the ovaries, causing skipped or irregular periods.

2. Excess follicle development:
Incomplete maturation: In PCOS, follicles begin to develop but fail to mature entirely, resulting in the production of tiny cysts in the ovaries. These cysts don't contain eggs and cannot be discharged.

Impact on ovulation: The existence of several cysts can hinder the dominant follicle from growing properly and releasing an egg, further adding to irregular periods.

3. Uterine lining changes:
Thickened lining: The hormonal imbalance might cause the uterine lining to thicken excessively.

Incomplete shedding: During menstruation, the thicker lining may not shed entirely, leading to increased bleeding, extended periods, or spotting between periods.

Irregular bleeding patterns: These alterations in the lining thickness and shedding lead to the unpredictable and irregular nature of periods in PCOS.

Additional factors:
Inflammation: Chronic low-grade inflammation, commonly linked with PCOS, can further affect hormone control and ovulation.

Genetics: PCOS has a hereditary component, meaning certain genes enhance the likelihood of having the illness.

Remember:
PCOS affects everyone differently, and the severity of menstrual irregularities might vary.

Understanding the underlying mechanisms will help you manage your PCOS and explore therapy choices for obtaining regular periods and enhancing reproductive potential.

Impact on Cycle Irregularity:

Symptoms: You may experience:
- Infrequent periods: Less than 8 cycles per year.

- Long cycles: Cycles surpassing 35 days.

- Unpredictable timing: Periods coming at varied intervals.

- Heavy or persistent bleeding: Due to the thickened uterine lining

- Spotting: Light bleeding between periods.

Managing PCOS and Irregular Cycles:

Lifestyle changes:
Healthy weight management: Losing even 5-10%
of body weight will increase insulin sensitivity
and ovulation.

Regular exercise: Moderate activity helps control
hormones and manage weight.

Balanced diet: Choose nutrient-rich meals and
limit processed sweets and harmful fats.

Stress management: Techniques like yoga,
meditation, and deep breathing might be useful.

Medications:
Hormonal birth control: Regulates cycles,
decreases testosterone levels, and improves skin
concerns.

Ovulation-inducing medications: Used to
encourage egg release for those trying to
conceive.

Insulin sensitizers: May be administered if insulin
resistance is evident.

Seeking Professional Help:

A healthcare practitioner can:
Diagnose PCOS using blood testing and ultrasound.

Discuss individualized treatment choices based on your requirements and goals.

Monitor your progress and change treatment as required.

Offer emotional support and direction.

Additional considerations to remember:
PCOS affects every woman differently, so there's no "one-size-fits-all" treatment.

Managing PCOS is a lifelong journey, but with the correct support and methods, you may have a healthy and full life.

Don't hesitate to seek further resources and support groups for information and community.

Understanding how irregular periods caused by PCOS affect your fertility journey can be immensely useful. Here's how we might examine this further:

Impact of PCOS on Fertility:
Reduced ovulation: As discussed before, PCOS can disrupt ovulation, making it harder to conceive naturally.

Egg quality: The hormonal imbalance might alter egg quality, thereby influencing fertilization and implantation success.

Other factors: PCOS can also contribute to other difficulties like insulin resistance, weight management challenges, and inflammation, which might indirectly impair fertility.

Fertility Options with PCOS:
Lifestyle changes: As noted previously, maintaining a healthy weight, exercising frequently, and managing stress can improve your general health and potentially enhance fertility.

Ovulation induction medication: These treatments stimulate the ovaries to release eggs, boosting your chances of pregnancy.

Intrauterine insemination (IUI): This method inserts sperm directly into the uterus, bypassing some reproductive problems.

In vitro fertilization (IVF): This method involves removing eggs, fertilizing them with sperm in a lab, and implanting the resulting embryos into the uterus.

Donor sperm or eggs: In some circumstances, utilizing donor sperm or eggs might be an option if your own eggs or partner's sperm are impacted.

Emotional Factors of Fertility in PCOS: Managing expectations: Irregular cycles can make it difficult to estimate ovulation and plan conception, leading to frustration and disappointment.

Facing societal pressures: Societal expectations around family planning can create additional stress and emotional strain.

Finding help: Connecting with other individuals with PCOS or fertility issues can offer essential emotional support and understanding.

Remember, navigating fertility issues with PCOS can be complex, and it's vital to seek tailored assistance from a healthcare practitioner specializing in reproductive endocrinology and infertility. They can examine your specific condition, discuss your fertility goals, and recommend the most suitable treatment alternatives for you.

3. Endometriosis

Endometriosis is a disorder when tissue comparable to the lining of the uterus (endometrium) grows outside the uterus. This displaced tissue can cause inflammation, discomfort, and fertility issues. Irregular periods are a typical sign of endometriosis, and they can make it difficult to get pregnant.

Here's how endometriosis can disrupt your reproductive journey:

Irregular ovulation:
Endometriosis can affect the usual hormonal balance in your body, which can lead to irregular ovulation. This means that you may not ovulate every month, or you may ovulate later than typical throughout your cycle.

Irregular ovulation is a critical worry associated with endometriosis and its impact on fertility. Here's how it works:

Endometriosis tissue releases inflammatory chemicals that can interfere with the connection between your brain (hypothalamus and pituitary gland) and ovaries.

This upsets the delicate balance of hormones needed for ovulation, namely:

Follicle-stimulating hormone (FSH): Stimulates egg formation in follicles.

Luteinizing hormone (LH): Triggers ovulation and development of the corpus luteum.

Estrogen and progesterone: Regulate the menstrual cycle and prepare the uterus for pregnancy.

Consequences of Irregular Ovulation:
Missed ovulation: You might not release an egg in certain months, making pregnancy difficult.

Late ovulation: This shortens the luteal phase (period after ovulation when pregnancy can occur), potentially limiting embryo implantation.

Unpredictable reproductive window: Makes it tougher to time intercourse or insemination for conception.

Understanding Your Cycle:
Tracking your menstrual cycle might assist discover ovulation trends and anomalies.

Tools like ovulation prediction kits (OPKs) or basal body temperature (BBT) charting can provide additional information.

Consulting a doctor for hormone testing can offer a more full picture.

Treatment Options:
Depending on the severity and individual instance, numerous treatment methods exist:

Hormonal therapies: Medications like birth control pills or GnRH agonists can regulate cycles and decrease endometriosis growth.

Surgery: Laparoscopic surgeries may remove endometriosis implants and increase ovulation potential.

Lifestyle modifications: Maintaining a healthy weight, reducing stress, and adopting a balanced diet can significantly improve hormone balance.

Remember:
Irregular ovulation is a frequent symptom of endometriosis, but it doesn't have to define your fertility journey.

Seek professional help to understand your individual circumstances and explore treatment alternatives that best suit you.

There are several tools and support groups available to navigate endometriosis and its complications.

Blocked fallopian tubes:
Endometriosis can also cause scar tissue to grow in your pelvic. This scar tissue can restrict your fallopian tubes, which are the tubes that deliver eggs from your ovaries to your uterus

Blocked fallopian tubes are a serious risk for fertility in patients with endometriosis. Here's some extra information on how endometriosis contributes to obstructed tubes and how it impacts fertility:

Mechanisms of blockage:
Direct obstruction: Endometrial tissue can grow inside the fallopian tubes, directly restricting the pathway for egg transport.

Adhesions: Scar tissue and adhesions caused by endometriosis can bind the fallopian tubes to surrounding tissues, altering their form and impeding egg migration.

Inflammation: Chronic inflammation can thicken the lining of the fallopian tubes, making it difficult for eggs to pass through.

Consequences of obstructed tubes:
Impeded fertilization: Blocked tubes prevent sperm from reaching the egg, making natural pregnancy impossible.

Increased ectopic pregnancy risk: If fertilization happens outside the fallopian tube, it's an ectopic pregnancy, a medical emergency.

Reduced choices for assisted reproduction: Depending on the severity of blockage, several assisted reproductive methods (ART) may not be an option.

Management strategies:
Surgery: Laparoscopic surgery can remove obstructions and adhesions, potentially restoring tubal patency.

Tubal recanalization: Minimally invasive techniques can sometimes reopen clogged tubes.

Assisted reproductive procedures (ART): Depending on the situation, IVF or other ART methods can bypass clogged tubes and achieve conception.

Additional items to consider:
The amount of tubal obstruction has a critical influence in treatment options and reproductive potential.

Early diagnosis and therapy of endometriosis can help prevent serious tubal damage.

Consulting a reproductive specialist is necessary to analyze the impact of blocked tubes on your unique scenario and discuss potential treatment choices.

Reduced egg quality:
Endometriosis can also impair the quality of your eggs. This is because the inflammation generated by endometriosis might harm your eggs.

The association between endometriosis and egg quality is complex and troubling for individuals seeking to conceive. Here's a deeper look at how endometriosis could affect egg quality:

Possible mechanisms of damage:
persistent inflammation: As you indicated, the persistent inflammatory environment induced by endometriosis can harm the DNA and mitochondria of eggs, reducing their health and viability.

Oxidative stress: The inflammation also generates free radicals, which can further harm egg quality.

Hormonal imbalances: Disrupted hormonal balance due to endometriosis may influence egg development and maturation.

Endometriomas: The presence of endometriomas (cysts) on the ovaries might potentially impede blood flow and oxygen availability, compromising egg health.

Consequences of lower egg quality:
Lower fertilization rates: Damaged eggs may not fertilize as readily, leading to diminished success with natural conception or assisted reproductive procedures (ART).

Increased miscarriage risk: Eggs with poor quality could have greater chromosomal abnormalities, increasing the risk of miscarriage.

Lower embryo quality: Even if fertilization occurs, damaged eggs may lead to embryos with lower implantation potential.

Current understanding and limitations:
While evidence reveals a link between endometriosis and egg quality, the exact processes are still being researched.

The severity of endometriosis and individual characteristics may alter the level of egg quality damage.

More study is needed to fully understand the connection and design focused solutions.

Management and considerations:
Early detection and treatment of endometriosis can potentially limit the influence on egg quality.

Lifestyle modifications including maintaining a healthy weight and controlling stress might contribute to increased egg health.

Consulting a fertility professional is vital to analyze your unique condition, address potential dangers, and explore fertility solutions.

Depending on your individual circumstances, ART treatments like IVF can be considered, where egg quality plays a vital role in treatment success.

It's crucial to note that even with endometriosis, many individuals obtain successful pregnancies. Consulting a healthcare practitioner and understanding your specific condition helps you to make informed decisions regarding your reproductive journey.

If you have endometriosis and are attempting to get pregnant, there are a number of things you may take to boost your chances:

See a doctor: It is crucial to see a doctor to discuss your endometriosis and obtain treatment. There are a number of therapies available, such as medication, surgery, and lifestyle modifications, that can help control your symptoms and increase your fertility.

Track your period: Tracking your cycle will help you spot any patterns in your ovulation. This information can be beneficial to your doctor when formulating a treatment plan.

Consider fertility treatments: If you are having problems getting pregnant on your own, you may want to consider fertility treatments such as in vitro fertilization (IVF).

Here are some extra strategies for controlling endometriosis and enhancing your fertility:

Maintain a healthy weight: Being overweight or obese might increase endometriosis symptoms and make it more difficult to get pregnant.

Eat a nutritious diet: Eating a healthy diet can help reduce inflammation and enhance your overall health.

Exercise regularly: Exercise can help relieve pain and enhance your general well-being.

Manage stress: Stress might increase endometriosis symptoms. Finding healthy strategies to manage stress might be useful.

If you are concerned about endometriosis and its impact on your fertility, talk to your doctor. They can help you build a plan to manage your condition and enhance your chances of getting pregnant.

4. How to Adjust Your Approach to Timing Intercourse if You Have Irregular Cycles

Having irregular cycles might make it difficult to tell when you are most fertile, and consequently when you are most likely to conceive. However, there are a few things you can do to change your approach to timing intercourse if you have irregular periods.

First, it is vital to track your menstrual periods. This can be done by utilizing a calendar, app, or chart. Tracking your periods can help you uncover patterns, such as the length of your cycle and the days you are most likely to ovulate. Once you have noticed these tendencies, you can start to arrange your relationship accordingly.

Second, you can utilize ovulation prediction kits (OPKs). OPKs detect a rise in luteinizing hormone (LH), which occurs soon before ovulation. Using OPKs can help you determine your most fertile days, which can boost your chances of conception.

Third, you can chat to your doctor. Your doctor can help you establish the reason for your irregular cycles and prescribe treatment choices. They can also help you establish a plan to maximize your chances of conception.

It is crucial to remember that everyone is different, and there is no one-size-fits-all method to scheduling intercourse. The best way to find a strategy that works for you is to talk to your doctor and experiment until you find what works best for you.

Understanding your cycle:

1. Tracking your cycle:

Apps: Numerous period monitoring applications exist, and many cater exclusively to irregular cycles. Look for features like:
Customizable cycle length input

Symptom logging, including cervical mucus changes, mood swings, and breast soreness

Ovulation prediction based on period history and symptoms (may not be accurate for irregular cycles)

Educational resources and community forums

Popular options include Flo, Clue, Glow, and Period Tracker by Planned Parenthood.

Calendar: Simple and free, but involves human data entry and calculations.
Mark period start and end dates, note significant symptoms, and utilize ovulation calculators online to predict your viable window (these may be less precise with irregular cycles).

2. Learning about ovulation:

Ovulation predictor kits (OPKs): Detect the LH surge before ovulation. Use daily around your estimated ovulation window, identified by period tracking or calendar methods. Follow kit instructions attentively for accurate results.

Cervical mucus observation: Requires regular monitoring of cervical mucus consistency and changes during your cycle. Mucus becomes transparent, elastic, and egg-white-like around ovulation. Requires practice and knowledge with your cycle.

Basal body temperature (BBT) charting: Requires taking your temperature first thing every morning before getting out of bed. A prolonged temperature rise of 0.5°F after ovulation proves ovulation happened. Can be cumbersome and demands commitment.

3. Consulting a fertility specialist:

Benefits: Personalized counsel, enhanced tests like hormone level checks and ultrasounds to pinpoint ovulation more precisely, addressing underlying reasons for irregular cycles.

Considerations: Cost, access, and personal preference.

Additional Tips:
Consistency is key: Whichever strategy you chose, use it consistently over multiple cycles to get insights.

Combine methods: For more accurate ovulation prediction consider combining two or more procedures like OPKs and BBT charting.

Seek expert aid when needed: Don't hesitate to visit a doctor or fertility specialist if you have worries about your cycle or problems conceiving.

Remember, understanding your cycle requires time and experimentation. Be patient, investigate multiple solutions, and seek expert help if needed.

Adjusting Your Approach:

1. Frequent intercourse: If you're not interested in pinpointing ovulation, having intercourse every other day throughout your cycle can enhance your chances of conceiving. This "shotgun" strategy doesn't need detecting ovulation but relies on having sex often enough to cover your whole reproductive window. This technique works best for couples with good sperm and no known reproductive difficulties.

Frequency: Aim for sex every other day during your cycle. This enhances the likelihood of sperm encountering an egg during ovulation, even if your cycle is erratic.

Benefits: Less stressful, requires no tracking or ovulation prediction, excellent for couples who love regular intercourse.

Drawbacks: Can be physically taxing, might not be perfect for budget limitations.

2. Focus on Fertile Window: If you're using OPKs or other ways to pinpoint ovulation, focus on having sex in the days preceding up to and including ovulation.
This tailored strategy utilizes ovulation prediction methods like OPKs, BBT charting, or ultrasound monitoring to pinpoint your viable window (1-2 days before ovulation and ovulation day itself).

Timing: Concentrate on having sex throughout your reproductive window. This maximizes the chances of conception while being less frequent than the "shotgun" technique.

Benefits: More efficient than frequent sex, decreases stress by focusing on specific days.

Drawbacks: Requires consistent tracking and ovulation prediction, might be stressful if ovulation timing varies greatly.

3. Alternative Methods: Sperm can survive in the female reproductive tract for up to 5 days, thus having intercourse even a few days before ovulation can still be beneficial.
This method uses the longevity of sperm (up to 5 days) to boost chances even if you can't identify ovulation accurately.

Timing: Have sex every 2-3 days throughout your cycle, starting a few days before your projected ovulation depending on your usual cycle length.

Benefits: Offers flexibility if ovulation timing is very unpredictable, less frequent than "shotgun" technique.

Drawbacks: Still requires some understanding of your cycle duration, could not be as effective as focusing on the viable window if ovulation occurs earlier or later than predicted.

Additional Tips:
Combine methods: Consider combining frequent intercourse with targeted attempts throughout your projected reproductive window for best outcomes.

Conversation: Open conversation with your partner about preferences and expectations can make trying to conceive more joyful and less stressful.

Relaxing: Stress can impact ovulation, so prioritize relaxing activities like meditation, yoga, or spending time in nature.

Seek Expert Help: If you've been trying for a year without success, visit a healthcare professional to rule out any underlying difficulties and obtain specialized assistance.

Remember, picking the best technique depends on your specific circumstances, tastes, and comfort level. Don't hesitate to experiment and change your plan based on your experiences and your doctor's assistance.

Additional Considerations:

1. Stress Management:
Impact on Cycle: Chronic stress can affect hormone control, resulting in irregular cycles, delayed ovulation, and even trouble conceiving.

Management Techniques:
Mindfulness and meditation: Practice deep breathing exercises, guided meditations, or mindfulness activities to quiet your mind and reduce stress hormones.

Physical activity: Regular exercise releases endorphins, natural mood-boosters that counteract stress. Choose activities you enjoy, like walking, swimming, or yoga.

Relaxation techniques: Explore gradual muscle relaxation, aromatherapy, or journaling to unwind and manage stress efficiently.

Seek Expert Help: If stress gets overwhelming, seek therapy or counseling to create coping mechanisms and manage stress long-term.

2. Healthy Lifestyle:
Balanced Diet: Nourish your body with whole foods including fruits, vegetables, whole grains, and lean protein. Limit processed foods, sugary drinks, and excessive coffee, which can severely disrupt hormonal balance.

Regular Exercise: Aim for at least 30 minutes of moderate-intensity exercise most days of the week. This helps regulate hormones, promote general health, and reduce stress.

Adequate Sleep: Aim for 7-8 hours of decent sleep each night. Sleep deprivation impairs hormonal homeostasis and can significantly impact ovulation.

Weight Management: Maintaining a healthy weight within your BMI range might promote general health and fertility. Consult your doctor

for specific assistance on healthy weight
management.

3. Open Communication:
Benefits: Talking openly with your spouse about
your cycle, expectations, and feelings can:

Reduce stress and worry associated with trying
to conceive.

Increase understanding and support for each
other.

Manage expectations and change tactics
collaboratively.

Communication Tips:
Share details about your cycle and any fertility
issues.

Express your feelings and expectations clearly
and honestly.

Actively listen to your partner's opinion and
concerns.

Discuss and agree on goals and tactics for
attempting to conceive.

Seek professional help if communication becomes difficult or distressing.

Remember:
These are general recommendations. Consult your doctor for specific advice and to address any underlying health concerns.

Combining these tactics can build a holistic approach to boost your chances of conception and manage stress during this journey.

Be patient, gentle to yourself, and seek support when required.

Remember, these are only broad guidelines, and the best strategy for you will depend on your unique circumstances. It's always advisable to consult with a healthcare expert for specific guidance.

Chapter Four:

Optimizing Your Chances of Conception

Embarking on the journey of parenthood is a thrilling and unique experience, filled with expectation and hopes for the future. However, for some couples, attempting to conceive can be a tough and sometimes stressful task. Fortunately, there are several actions you can take to enhance your chances of conception, producing a more informed and empowered approach to this crucial life event.

The basis for optimal conception depends on understanding your menstrual cycle.
This involves:

Tracking: Regularly tracking your period start and end dates helps detect patterns and potential ovulation windows. Apps like Flo and Clue can assist in this process.

Ovulation: While normally happening about 14 days before your next period, unpredictable cycles demand alternate methods like ovulation predictor kits (OPKs) or basal body temperature (BBT) charting.

Seeking Professional Help: If you have concerns or irregular cycles, consulting a doctor or fertility specialist can provide specific counsel and rule out any underlying difficulties.

Optimizing Your Health: Both partners' overall health plays a key impact in fertility:

Diet: Opt for a balanced diet rich in fruits, vegetables, whole grains, and lean protein, while reducing processed foods, sugary drinks, and excessive caffeine.

Exercise: Regular moderate-intensity exercise enhances hormonal balance and stress management. Aim for at least 30 minutes most days of the week.

Sleep: Prioritize 7-8 hours of excellent sleep each night to promote optimal hormone regulation.

Weight Management: Maintaining a healthy weight within your BMI range enhances general health and fertility. Consult your doctor for specific advice.

Stress Management: Chronic stress can disrupt your cycle and negatively damage fertility. Here are some effective strategies:

Mindfulness & Meditation: Deep breathing, guided meditations, and mindfulness activities can quiet the mind and lower stress hormones.

Physical Activity: Regular exercise releases endorphins, natural mood-boosters that counteract stress. Find activities you enjoy, like walking, swimming, or yoga.

Relaxation Techniques: Explore progressive muscle relaxation, aromatherapy, or journaling to unwind and manage stress effectively.

Seek Professional Help: If managing stress feels overwhelming, therapy or counseling can equip you with coping methods and long-term stress management skills.

Adjusting Your Approach:
Once you have a better grasp of your cycle and health, you can change your approach to sex to enhance your chances:

Frequency: For couples with no known reproductive concerns, having intercourse every other day throughout your cycle (shotgun technique) boosts sperm-egg encounter odds.

Fertile Window: Utilizing OPKs, BBT charting, or ultrasound monitoring to define your fertile window (1-2 days before ovulation and ovulation day) enables for targeted efforts during the most opportune time frame.

Alternative Methods: Considering sperm's longevity (up to 5 days), having sex every 2-3 days throughout your cycle, starting a few days before your projected ovulation, can be beneficial even with irregular cycles.

Open Communication:
Talking freely with your partner about your cycle, expectations, and feelings can substantially improve the experience:

Reducing Stress: Sharing concerns and anxieties can decrease stress and develop support for one other.

Managing Expectations: Discussing individual and shared goals helps adapt plans and manage expectations together.

Seeking Support: If communication becomes problematic, try couples therapy to address concerns and enhance communication skills.

Additional Resources and Support:

The American Society for Reproductive Medicine (ASRM)

The National Infertility Association (NIA)

Resolve: The National Infertility Association

Online forums and support groups exclusively for couples attempting to conceive

Remember:
This material serves as a general guide. Consult your doctor for specific advice and to address any underlying health concerns.

Optimizing your chances of conception is a holistic approach, embracing your physical and mental well-being. Be patient, gentle to yourself, and don't hesitate to seek professional support when needed.

The route to motherhood is unique for every couple. Embrace the process, appreciate minor wins, and remember, you are not alone.

I hope the following empowers you on your quest towards conception. May it be filled with education, wisdom, and ultimately, the joy of welcome new life into your family.

1. The Best Time to Have Intercourse for Pregnancy

Unfortunately, there's no single "best time" for everyone to have intercourse for pregnancy. The optimal timing depends largely on your unique cycle, and various factors come into play. However, let us look at the essential things to consider and how to maximize your chances of conception.

Tracking Your Cycle:
This is vital. Use cycle tracking apps or simply mark your calendar to spot patterns and probable ovulation windows.

Period Tracker Apps:

Flo: Offers cycle prediction, tailored insights, and instructional content.

Clue: Focuses on data privacy and includes symptom tracking and community forums.

Glow: Includes fertility education, couple synchronizing, and ovulation prediction based on symptoms and period history.

Period Tracker by Planned Parenthood: Free, dependable tool with basic tracking capabilities and educational resources.

Consider: Look for features like adjustable cycle length input, symptom logging, ovulation prediction (may be less precise for irregular periods), and educational materials.

Beyond Apps:q
Calendar Method: Simple and free, requires manual data entry and calculations. Mark period start and end dates, note relevant symptoms, and use online ovulation calculators (less accurate with irregular cycles).

Basal Body Temperature (BBT) Charting: Requires taking your temperature first thing every morning before getting out of bed. A prolonged temperature rise of 0.5°F after ovulation proves ovulation happened. Can be cumbersome and demands commitment.

Cervical Mucus Observation: Requires regular monitoring of cervical mucus consistency and changes during your cycle. Mucus becomes transparent, elastic, and egg-white-like around ovulation. Requires practice and knowledge with your cycle.

Irregular Cycles: Special Considerations:
If your periods are irregular, pinpointing ovulation becomes tougher. Consider ovulation predictor kits (OPKs), basal body temperature (BBT) tracking, or visiting a doctor for specialized help.

Apps: Many period monitoring apps cater to irregular cycles with features like:

Irregularity tracking and adjustment of projections based on past cycles.

More flexible cycle length input options.

Integration with other tracking methods like BBT.

OPKs: Use consistently around your projected ovulation window (determined by period tracking app or other means) to identify the LH rise.

Combine procedures: For more accurate ovulation prediction, consider combining two or more procedures like OPKs and BBT charting.

Doctor Consultation: Don't hesitate to visit a doctor or fertility specialist if you have concerns about your cycle or problems conceiving. They can offer tailored assistance, advanced tests including hormone level checks and ultrasounds, and address underlying health issues.

Ovulation:
This is when you're most fertile, often around 14 days before your next menstruation. But knowing yours specifically is key.

Timing: While typically 14 days before your next period, this can vary.

Additional signs:
Cervical mucus changes: Becomes transparent, stretchy, and egg-white-like around ovulation. Requires observation and practice.

Basal body temperature (BBT): A modest increase in temperature suggests ovulation has occurred. Requires taking your temperature first thing in the morning before getting out of bed, daily throughout your cycle.

Ovulation discomfort (mittelschmerz): Some suffer modest pelvic pain around ovulation.

Additional Tips:
Consistency is key: Whichever strategy you choose, do it regularly for several cycles to get insights.

Be patient: It can take time to understand your cycle, especially with irregular periods.

Seek expert help: Don't hesitate to visit your doctor if you have concerns or problems determining ovulation.

Trust your body: Pay attention to your body's signals and small changes throughout your cycle.

Track additional symptoms: Logging cervical mucus changes, mood swings, breast soreness, and other changes might help find patterns and refine your forecast.

Seek support: Talk to your partner, family, or online forums for understanding and encouragement throughout your journey.

Remember, understanding your cycle is a critical aspect in optimizing your chances of conception. By using multiple tracking methods, researching additional symptoms, and seeking expert advice when needed, you can get useful insights about your individual reproductive window.

Maximizing Your Chances:

Focus on the Fertile Window:
Sperm Survival: While an egg survives for roughly 24 hours, sperm can survive up to 5 days in your body. This gives you a window of opportunity.

Targeted Efforts: Use OPKs, BBT, or ultrasound to identify your viable window (1-2 days before ovulation and ovulation day itself). Aim for sex during this window for the maximum odds.

Alternative Approaches:
Frequent intercourse: If pinpointing ovulation is problematic, consider having intercourse every other day throughout your cycle (shotgun approach). This enhances the likelihood of sperm encountering an egg, even with irregular periods.

Flexibility: If your ovulation time changes greatly, having intercourse every 2-3 days throughout your cycle, starting a few days before your projected ovulation, can still be helpful.

Consider These Factors:
Stress: Chronic stress can disrupt your cycle, so prioritizing relaxation practices like meditation, yoga, or exercise is vital.

Lifestyle: A balanced diet, regular exercise, and proper sleep are vital for general health and can indirectly boost fertility.

Open Communication: Talking freely with your spouse about your cycle, expectations, and concerns can dramatically reduce stress and make the process more joyful.

Remember:
This is generic information. Consult your doctor for specific advice and to rule out any underlying health concerns.

Be patient and nice to yourself. Conception can take time, so celebrate tiny accomplishments and don't hesitate to seek expert support if needed.

There is no one-size-fits-all method. Experiment, change techniques based on your experiences, and remember, you are not alone in this path.

Beyond the Basics: Advanced Strategies for Optimizing Conception

While understanding your cycle and timing intercourse around ovulation are vital, numerous advanced tactics can further boost your chances of conception:

Advanced Fertility Tracking:
Cervical Mucus Observation: Monitoring variations in cervical mucus consistency throughout your cycle can assist pinpoint ovulation. Look for clear, stretchy, egg-white-like mucus around ovulation.

Ultrasound Monitoring: Your doctor can use ultrasound to track follicle development and precisely detect ovulation. This is beneficial for irregular cycles or specific fertility difficulties.

Lifestyle Tweaks:
Supplements: Consult your doctor about prenatal vitamins for both couples, as some studies suggest they could boost egg and sperm quality.

Caffeine Moderation: Limit caffeine intake to moderate levels (less than 200 mg daily), since high intake can influence fertility in both men and women.

Lubricant Selection: Avoid lubricants with spermicide, as they can destroy sperm. Water-based lubricants are safe and effective.

Partner Health:
Male Fertility: Encourage your partner to keep healthy habits including frequent exercise, balanced diet, and stress management. Sperm quality can substantially affect fertilization.

Pre-existing Conditions: If either spouse has any pre-existing medical conditions, visit your doctor to ensure they're controlled well and not hurting fertility.

Beyond Intercourse:
Fertility Specialist: If you've been trying for a year without success, visit a fertility specialist. They can give modern tests, treatments like intrauterine insemination (IUI) or in vitro fertilization (IVF), and tailored coaching.

Emotional Support: Trying to conceive can be emotionally hard. Consider marital therapy or attending support groups to handle stress and connect with others having similar difficulties.

Additional considerations:
Sexual positions: While no one position assures conception, some couples find various positions more comfortable or beneficial. Explore and see what works best for you.

Timing intercourse: Aim for climax for both partners, since it may boost sperm quality and cervical mucus composition.

Mindset and emotional well-being:
Managing stress: Utilize relaxation techniques like meditation, yoga, or deep breathing exercises to reduce tension and anxiety, which can negatively affect fertility.

Positive affirmations: Focusing on positive ideas and beliefs regarding conception helps generate a more helpful mental environment.

Support network: Surround yourself with sympathetic friends, family members, or online communities who understand your struggle and can offer encouragement.

Remember:
The information in this book is not a substitute for expert medical advice. Always visit your doctor for individualized recommendations based

on your specific circumstances and health history.

The route to conception might be unique and may take long. Be patient, supportive of each other, and enjoy every milestone along the road.

There is no single "magic bullet" for getting pregnant. Combining a healthy lifestyle, smart scheduling techniques, and open communication can dramatically boost your chances of success.

Remember, this information serves as a starting point, and individual requirements and situations differ. Consulting your doctor or a fertility specialist is vital to build a specific plan and address any underlying health concerns. Be patient, nice to yourself, and appreciate every milestone on this path.

2. Intercourse Frequency for Conception: A Balancing Act

When it comes to intercourse frequency and conception, there's no one-size-fits-all answer. The "best" strategy varies on various aspects, including your cycle regularity and personal preferences. However, here's some general knowledge to aid you:

The Science Behind Sperm & Eggs:

Sperm lifespan: Sperm can live in the female reproductive tract for up to 5 days.

Egg lifespan: An egg generally lives for around 24 hours following ovulation.

Two Main Approaches:
1. Shot-gun Approach: Frequency: Aim for sex every other day throughout your period.

Benefit: This maximizes sperm presence, improving the possibility of sperm encountering an egg, even with erratic cycles.

Drawbacks: Can be physically hard and demands continual effort, perhaps hurting spontaneity.

2. Fertile Window Approach:
Identify fertile window: Use tools like ovulation prediction kits (OPKs), basal body temperature (BBT) charting, or ultrasound monitoring to identify your 1-2 days before ovulation and ovulation day itself.

Focus efforts: Aim for intercourse within your fertile window to optimize the chances of fertilization.

Benefits: Less frequent than the shot-gun technique, potentially less physically demanding, targets the most optimum moment for conception.

Drawbacks: Requires accurate ovulation prediction, may not be suited for everyone, especially with extremely variable ovulation timing.

Alternative Approach:
Moderate approach: Have sex every 2-3 days throughout your cycle, starting a few days before your predicted ovulation.

Benefit: Offers flexibility, accommodates irregular cycles, still leverages sperm longevity advantage.

Drawback: Less targeted than the fruitful window approach.

Additional Considerations:
Stress: Chronic stress can affect your cycle and sperm quality, so emphasize stress management with relaxing strategies.

Lifestyle: Healthy habits including balanced food, frequent exercise, and appropriate sleep contribute to overall health and can boost fertility.

Open communication: Discussing preferences and expectations with your spouse can minimize tension and make the experience more enjoyable.

Remember: This information is for general knowledge only. Consult your doctor for specific advice and to address any underlying health concerns.

Experiment and change your strategy based on your experiences and comfort level.
There is no sure formula for conception. Be patient, nice to yourself, and seek professional support when needed.

By understanding your cycle, exploring multiple options, and emphasizing overall well-being, you can construct an informed and empowering path towards conception.
Let us discuss more issues and considerations:

Optimizing Timing Within Your Fertile Window:

Multiple times inside your fertile window: While having intercourse once during the window is sufficient, some studies suggest higher frequency (e.g., every other day) may modestly improve odds.

Specific timing: While no solid proof exists for a "best" moment inside the window, some couples find morning sex more beneficial due to better sperm motility. Ultimately, the timing that works best for you and your spouse is crucial.

Factors Affecting Sperm Quality and Quantity:

Frequency of ejaculation: Frequent ejaculations (daily) can diminish sperm count and quality, while abstinence for longer than 3-4 days may impact motility. Aiming for a moderate frequency of 2-3 times a week seems optimal. While more frequent ejaculations can initially decrease sperm count, research suggests this is transitory and rebounds within a few days. Regular, but not excessive, ejaculations can potentially improve sperm quality.

Lifestyle: Smoking, heavy alcohol usage, and recreational drugs might severely affect sperm health. Prioritizing a healthy lifestyle enhances overall fertility.

Abstinence: Contrary to widespread assumption, long durations of abstinence (more than 7 days) might not significantly increase sperm quality.

Other factors: Stress, lifestyle behaviors (smoking, excessive alcohol), and some drugs might significantly affect sperm health. Address these elements for optimal sperm production.

Tailoring Your Approach:
Cycle regularity: If your cycles are regular, the fertile window strategy may be more beneficial.

Sperm analysis: If your spouse has low sperm count or motility, discuss with your doctor if adjusting frequency or investigating alternative options like assisted reproductive technologies (ART) is necessary.

Personal preferences: Choose a strategy that matches with your comfort level and emotional well-being.

Advanced Techniques:
Sperm analysis: This can provide vital information into sperm health and influence your approach.

Ovulation monitoring: Using ultrasound or other technologies for exact ovulation timing might further improve your efforts.
Post-coital testing: This can detect sperm presence and motility in the cervical mucus after intercourse.

Additional Approaches to Consider:
Post-coital positioning: Lying down for 15-20 minutes after intercourse may marginally boost sperm reaching the cervix. However, the evidence for this is minimal and comfort should be prioritized.

Orgasms: While not needed for conception, orgasms might potentially increase cervical mucus and sperm movement.

Note:
These are extra insights, not assurances of success.

This material is not a substitute for expert medical advice. Consult your doctor for individualized recommendations based on your specific situation.

Individual considerations such as underlying medical issues or age may require further examination and personalized recommendations from your doctor.

Open communication and collaborative decision-making with your partner are vital in navigating this path together.

Emotional Well-being and Stress:
Stress management: Chronic stress can adversely impair both male and female fertility. Incorporate relaxation practices like meditation, yoga, or deep breathing into your regimen.

Positive mindset: Focusing on positive affirmations and maintaining a hopeful outlook can produce a more helpful atmosphere for conception.

Seeking professional help: If stress becomes overwhelming, consider therapy or counseling to establish healthy coping techniques.

Embrace the Journey:
Celebrate small victories: Track your progress and acknowledge each step along the way.

Manage expectations: Conception might take time, so be patient and nice to yourself.

Seek support: Surround yourself with sympathetic friends, family, or online communities that understand your struggle and can offer encouragement.

By understanding your biology, enhancing your health, and controlling stress are critical parts of creating a healthy environment for conception. By exploring multiple techniques, receiving professional help when needed, and prioritizing your mental well-being, you can empower yourself and your partner on this path towards motherhood.

3. Intercourse Positions For Conception

It's crucial to note that while there are many misconceptions and beliefs regarding specific intercourse positions for conception, there is no scientific evidence to support the idea that any single position greatly boosts your chances of conceiving. Sperm are highly efficient swimmers, and once deposited in the vagina, they are capable of reaching the egg regardless of the posture utilized.

However, there are several general aspects that could help to a more comfortable and potentially more joyful experience during intercourse:

Regarding intercourse positions:

Gravity: While some believe gravity has a role, research reveals sperm are excellent swimmers and can reach the egg regardless of position.

Comfort and enjoyment: Choose a position that feels comfortable and delightful for both partners. Stress and discomfort can significantly affect the experience and potentially hinder fertility.

Experimentation: Explore and find positions that allow for deep penetration, which can improve the possibility of sperm reaching the cervix.

Communicate with your partner about preferences and adapt as needed.

Sperm survival:

While sperm can survive for up to 5 days in the female reproductive canal, postures with deeper penetration might help them to reach the cervix faster, thus providing them a tiny edge.

However, this is a very minor component, and focusing mostly on comfort and relaxation is more significant.

Additional considerations:

Lubricants: Avoid spermicidal lubricants, as they harm sperm. Opt for water-based lubricants if needed.

Orgasms: While not needed for conception, orgasms can potentially boost sperm quality and cervical mucus composition, making it simpler for sperm to migrate.

Consult your doctor: If you have any concerns or unique health conditions that might influence your choice of postures, visit your doctor for tailored advice.

Important factors to remember:

The most significant elements for conception are healthy sperm and egg, ovulation timing, and overall health.

Don't place extra pressure on yourselves or focus on specific positions as the key to success.

Enjoy the process, communicate openly, and promote relaxation and well-being.

Focus on overall health: Prioritize good nutrition, regular exercise, stress management, and appropriate sleep for both spouses.

Pinpoint your reproductive window: Utilize ovulation tracking methods to enhance your chances.

Consult a doctor: If you've been trying for a year without success, seek professional help to rule out any underlying difficulties

While choosing the "best" intercourse position for conception could sound enticing, it's crucial to note that there's no specific position guaranteed to boost your chances. Conception is influenced by various variables, including:

Sperm quality and quantity: Healthy sperm with adequate motility are crucial contributors.

Prioritize overall wellness and treat any underlying concerns that can impair sperm health.

Timing: Having intercourse during your reproductive window (1-2 days before ovulation and ovulation day itself) is key.

Utilize methods like ovulation predictor kits or basal body temperature charting to pinpoint this window.

Cervical mucus: Favorable cervical mucus consistency (clear, flexible, egg-white-like) permits sperm to migrate more freely.

Stress management and healthy lifestyle practices can contribute to this.

Remember, conception is a natural process, and concentrating on general well-being and informed methods will produce a more positive and empowered experience on your journey towards parenting.

4. Factors Affecting Conception

While timing intercourse around ovulation plays a significant role, conception is a complex process influenced by several factors beyond the immediate act. Here's a detailed look at some significant contributors:

Biological factors:

Age: Female fertility drops dramatically after the mid-30s due to decreasing egg quality and quantity. Sperm quality in men likewise drops with age, though at a slower rate.

Medical problems: Several medical issues can impair fertility in both men and women. In women, endometriosis, Polycystic Ovary Syndrome (PCOS), and obstructed fallopian tubes are significant issues. Men could experience issues due to poor sperm count, varicocele (enlarged veins around the testicles), or hormonal imbalances.

Genetics: Certain genetic abnormalities can influence sperm production or egg quality, resulting in infertility.

Reproductive history: Previous sexually transmitted infections (STIs) or pelvic procedures can potentially cause harm to reproductive organs, reducing fertility.

Biological Factors Affecting Conception:

Female factors:

Ovulation: This is an important biological event, releasing a developed egg from the ovary each month. Irregular or absent ovulation can greatly affect conception. Factors like hormone imbalances, PCOS, and stress can affect ovulation.

Egg quality: Egg quality falls with age, lowering the chances of fertilization and healthy implantation. Genetic problems and some medical treatments can also affect egg quality.

Cervical mucus: This mucus plays a key function in sperm survival and transit towards the fallopian tubes. Certain drugs, illnesses, or hormonal imbalances might change the quality or quantity of cervical mucus, limiting sperm motility.

Fallopian tubes: These tubes convey the egg from the ovary to the uterus. Blockages due to scar tissue from pelvic surgery, infections, or endometriosis can prevent fertilization from occurring.

Uterine lining: The endometrium, the lining of the uterus, needs to be receptive for implantation of a fertilized egg. Hormonal abnormalities, thin lining, or uterine fibroids can hamper effective implantation.

Male factors:

Sperm production: Sperm production occurs in the testicles and can be influenced by causes like varicocele, hormonal imbalances, hereditary disorders, and infections.

Sperm quality: This comprises parameters like sperm count, motility (movement), and morphology (shape). Low sperm count, poor motility, or aberrant morphology can lower the odds of fertilization.

Ejaculation: Erectile dysfunction, early ejaculation, or poor semen volume might limit sperm transport to the cervix, influencing conception.

Additional points:

Immune system issues: In rare circumstances, the immune system may assault sperm, limiting fertilization.

Undiagnosed medical issues: Certain underlying medical conditions, such thyroid disorders or diabetes, can impair fertility in both men and women.

Lifestyle factors:

Weight: Being overweight or underweight can disturb hormonal balance and ovulation in women, while obesity might decrease sperm quality in men.

Diet: A balanced diet rich in fruits, vegetables, and whole grains is necessary for good reproductive health. Conversely, shortages in important vitamins and minerals might impair fertility.

Exercise: While moderate exercise is good, excessive physical activity might disrupt menstruation cycles and ovulation in women.

Substance use: Smoking, heavy alcohol intake, and recreational drug use can drastically impair both male and female fertility.

Stress: Chronic stress can boost cortisol levels, which might interfere with ovulation and sperm production.

Environmental factors:

Exposure to toxins: Certain environmental pollutants, such as pesticides and heavy metals, can significantly affect sperm quality and egg health.

Occupational hazards: Some activities expose persons to radiation, heat, or other toxic substances that can impact fertility.

Psychological factors:

Stress: As discussed before, persistent stress can impair conception.

Anxiety and depression: These mental health issues can disrupt hormonal balance and sexual function, impacting fertility.

Other factors:

Frequency of intercourse: While there's no "magic number," having sex every 2-3 days around ovulation can boost the odds of conceiving.

Lubricants: Certain lubricants can be spermicidal, lowering sperm viability. Choosing water-based or sperm-friendly lubricants is suggested.

Remember:

This information is for general understanding only and does not represent medical advice. If you're concerned about your fertility, please visit a healthcare professional for specialized assistance and evaluation.

Chapter Five:

Lifestyle Factors That Can Improve Fertility

Conceiving a child is a journey filled with expectation, excitement, and occasionally, frustration. While biology plays a key part, the path to motherhood can be considerably altered by the decisions we make in our everyday lives. That's where lifestyle factors come into play, acting as hidden keys that can unlock the door to fertility.

This chapter will look into the particular ways our nutrition, exercise habits, stress levels, and even environmental exposures can affect our capacity to conceive. We'll expose the science behind these relationships, empowering you to make informed decisions that optimize your chances of welcoming a new life. Remember, taking control of your lifestyle isn't just about ticking boxes; it's about establishing a holistic environment that supports maximum health and well-being, setting the stage for a healthy pregnancy and a joyful journey into parenting.

So, whether you're currently trying to conceive or simply exploring your possibilities for the future, this exploration will provide you with vital insights and actionable strategies. Let's uncover the possibilities within your lifestyle choices and build the way for a brighter, fertile future.

1. Diet and Exercise: The Powerhouse Duo for Boosting Fertility

The road to fertility isn't merely paved with medical interventions; it's also highly influenced by the everyday choices we make regarding our diet and activity. These lifestyle factors interact with our bodies in fundamental ways, altering hormone levels, egg and sperm quality, and overall reproductive health. Let's go deeper into how each plays a key role:

Diet:

A balanced diet rich in fruits, vegetables, whole grains, lean proteins, and healthy fats supplies the required elements for normal reproductive function. These include:

Folic acid: Found in leafy greens and legumes, it lessens the chance of birth abnormalities.

Antioxidants: Present in colored fruits and vegetables, they counteract free radicals that destroy eggs and sperm.

Healthy fats: Monounsaturated and polyunsaturated lipids, found in olive oil, almonds, and avocados, boost hormone production and egg quality.

Iron: Important for egg formation and ovulation, found in red meat, lentils, and fortified cereals.

Mindful Eating: Processed meals, excessive sugar, and bad fats contribute to inflammation and hormone imbalances, limiting fertility. Opting for a whole-food, well-balanced approach is crucial.

Tailoring for Specific Needs: Individual dietary needs may differ based on existing health issues or PCOS diagnosis. Consulting a licensed dietitian experienced with fertility concerns can be quite beneficial.

Exercise:

Regular moderate-intensity exercise (30 minutes most days of the week) enhances egg and sperm quality, controls menstrual cycles, and optimizes hormonal balance. Activities like brisk walking, swimming, and cycling are ideal possibilities.

Finding the Sweet Spot: Excessive exercise can be detrimental, exerting stress on the body and altering hormones. Aim for moderation and listen to your body's instincts.

Tailoring Activity Levels: For those with current health concerns or particular needs, consulting a healthcare practitioner can help build a safe and effective fitness program that supports fertility.

The Synergistic Effect: The genuine magic lies in the combined power of a good diet and regular exercise. They work synergistically, boosting each other's benefits:

Weight Management: Maintaining a healthy weight is vital for fertility. Both nutrition and exercise contribute to reaching and maintaining a healthy BMI, which enhances hormonal balance and ovulation regularity.

Stress Reduction: Both hobbies are natural stress relievers, which is vital for fertility as persistent stress can impair ovulation and sperm production.

Improved Blood Flow: Exercise increases healthy blood flow, enabling crucial nutrients to reach reproductive organs for maximum function.
Remember:
Individualized Approach: Consult your doctor or a reproductive specialist to understand your individual needs and adapt these advice accordingly.

Consistency is Key: Making small, sustained modifications to your food and exercise habits over time will bring the most substantial effects.

Seek Support: Don't hesitate to seek support from healthcare professionals, dietitians, or fertility counselors for individualized guidance and inspiration.

By harnessing the power of nutrition and exercise, you may create a fertile foundation for conception and set the way for a successful pregnant journey. Remember, it's about empowering yourself with knowledge and making informed decisions that nurture your body and enhance your chances of receiving a little miracle into your life.

Diet: Food Powerhouses for Fertility:

Fruits & Vegetables: Go rainbow! Aim for at least 5 servings daily, focusing on antioxidant-rich berries, citrus fruits, leafy greens, and cruciferous veggies like broccoli and cauliflower. Whole Grains: Opt for brown rice, quinoa, oats, and whole-wheat bread for sustained energy and fiber, which promotes digestion and hormone balance.

Lean Proteins: Include fish (salmon, tuna) rich in Omega-3 fatty acids, poultry, beans, lentils, and tofu for important amino acids that form healthy eggs and sperm.

Healthy Fats: Embrace olive oil, avocado, almonds, and seeds for vital fatty acids that boost hormone production and egg quality.

Fermented Foods: Yogurt, kefir, kimchi, and sauerkraut boost gut health, which impacts hormone balance and overall well-being.
Foods to Limit:

Processed Foods: Limit processed meats, fizzy drinks, refined carbohydrates (white bread, spaghetti), and unhealthy fats (trans fats, saturated fats) as they contribute to inflammation and hormonal imbalances.

Caffeine: Moderate coffee intake (1-2 cups per day) is typically regarded as safe, but excessive consumption can disturb sleep and ovulation.

Alcohol: Excessive alcohol use might significantly damage egg and sperm quality. Moderate intake is key.

Individualized Considerations:
PCOS: Focus on regulating insulin levels with a low-glycemic diet rich in fruits, vegetables, and whole grains. Consider consulting a nutritionist specializing in PCOS.

Endometriosis: Reduce inflammation with a diet rich in fruits, vegetables, and omega-3 fatty acids while restricting red meat and dairy.

Exercise: Moving for Fertility:
Variety is Key: Mix up things you enjoy like brisk walking, swimming, cycling, dancing, or yoga to stay motivated and minimize monotony.

High-Intensity Interval Training (HIIT): Short bursts of intense activity followed by rest periods can be good in modest doses, but consult your doctor before commencing HIIT.

Strength Training: Include moderate strength training activities 2-3 times a week to build muscle mass, which improves metabolism and hormone balance.

Tailoring Your Approach:
Pregnant or Breastfeeding: Consult your doctor for particular suggestions as exercise needs change during and after pregnancy.

Existing Health Conditions: Adapt your workout regimen based on your doctor's advice to ensure safety and efficacy.

Remember:
Listen to Your Body: Rest when needed and avoid pushing yourself to fatigue.

Start progressively: Begin with brief workouts and progressively increase duration and intensity over time.

Find a Support System: Join a fitness class or locate a workout buddy for encouragement and accountability.

Additional Tips:
Manage Stress: Practice yoga, meditation, deep breathing, or spending time in nature to reduce stress and promote hormonal balance.

Stay Hydrated: Drink enough water throughout the day to keep your body functioning effectively. Consider Supplementation: Consult your doctor about prenatal vitamins or particular supplements to address any deficits.

Remember:
While these are broad tips, it's vital to visit your doctor or a fertility specialist for specific guidance based on your unique health and circumstances. By making informed choices regarding your nutrition and exercise, you're taking a proactive step towards enhancing your odds of conception and welcoming a healthy pregnancy.

2. Stress Management: The Unsung Hero of Fertility Enhancement

While often disregarded, stress management merits a prominent role in the fertility drama. Chronic stress is a quiet saboteur, affecting delicate hormone balances and limiting the optimum functioning of your reproductive system. Let's study how implementing stress management strategies might drastically boost your chances of conception:

The Physiology of Stress and Fertility:

When stressed, your body releases cortisol, the "fight-or-flight" hormone. While useful in acute instances, prolonged cortisol increase wreaks havoc on fertility:

Disrupts Ovulation: Cortisol can interfere with the complicated hormonal dance that leads to egg release, making ovulation sporadic or unpredictable.

Reduces Sperm Quality: In men, increased cortisol can decrease sperm count, motility, and morphology, reducing their ability to reach and fertilize the egg.

Thins the Uterine Lining: High cortisol levels can impair the thickness of the uterine lining, required for embryo implantation and a successful pregnancy.

Lowers Libido: Stress can decrease sexual desire and closeness, further hampering conception efforts.

Stress Management Techniques for Fertility Boost:

Fortunately, we can empower ourselves to resist stress and maximize our fertility by embracing these effective practices:

Mindfulness & Meditation: Techniques like mindful breathing, guided meditations, and progressive muscular relaxation encourage your mind to focus on the present moment, minimizing stress response and encouraging relaxation.

Yoga and Tai Chi: These mind-body activities combine moderate exercise with deep breathing and mindfulness, delivering a holistic approach to stress reduction and better body awareness.

Physical Activity: Regular moderate exercise like brisk walking, swimming, or cycling produces endorphins, the body's natural mood lifters, and helps handle stress effectively.

Connecting with Nature: Spending time in nature, whether wandering through a park or simply sitting amidst greenery, has been demonstrated to lower stress levels and enhance general well-being.

Creative Expression: Activities like writing, painting, or dancing assist you to process emotions and channel stress in a healthy way.

Social Support: Surround yourself with loved ones who are supportive and understanding of your fertility journey. Sharing your problems and experiences can alleviate stress and provide emotional encouragement.

Making it Personalized:

There's no one-size-fits-all method to stress management. Discover what works best for you by trying with different strategies and discovering activities you actually enjoy. Consistency is crucial, so integrate these routines into your regular routine to enjoy their cumulative advantages.

Additional Tips:

Identify Your Stressors: Pinpoint the situations or individuals that create stress in your life and develop techniques to manage them effectively.

Set Realistic Expectations: Accept that conception can take time and avoid putting unnecessary pressure on yourself or your partner.

Seek Professional Help: If you're struggling to manage stress on your own, consider seeking advice from a therapist or counselor specialized in stress management or reproductive concerns. Remember:
Reducing stress isn't just about getting pregnant; it's about developing a healthier, happier version of yourself. By making stress management a priority, you're taking a proactive step towards not just raising your fertility but also enhancing your general well-being and providing a strong foundation for a successful pregnancy and joyous motherhood.

The Physiological Cascade:

Understanding the complicated dance of hormones under stress is vital. When faced with a stressor, the hypothalamus prompts the adrenal glands to release cortisol. While useful in short bursts, persistent cortisol increase affects the reproductive system:

Hypothalamic-Pituitary-Gonadal Axis (HPG) Disruption: This axis orchestrates hormone production during ovulation and menstruation.

Chronically high cortisol reduces Gonadotropin-Releasing Hormone (GnRH), leading to diminished Follicle-Stimulating Hormone (FSH) and Luteinizing Hormone (LH). This domino effect impairs egg development, ovulation regularity, and endometrial lining thickness, impeding implantation.

Sex Hormone Imbalance: Stress boosts cortisol and prolactin (the "milk hormone"), influencing estrogen and progesterone synthesis. This imbalance can lead to irregular cycles, diminished cervical mucus (important for sperm migration), and possibly early loss.

Sperm Damage: Cortisol directly affects sperm production, motility, and morphology. Studies demonstrate lower sperm count, impaired swimming ability, and aberrant shape in males undergoing chronic stress, limiting fertilization chances.

Beyond Physiology: The Mind-Body Connection:

Stress effects fertility not simply through hormones, but also through psychological factors:

Decreased Libido: Chronic stress can diminish sexual desire and intimacy, making conception less likely.

Performance Anxiety: The urge to conceive might induce performance anxiety, further hampering relaxation and enjoyment during sex.

Negative Emotions: Stress typically causes worry, despair, and frustration, generating emotional pressure that can significantly affect general health and well-being.

Tailored Stress Management Strategies:

The good news? You have the power to alleviate stress and boost your fertility potential:

Mindfulness & Meditation: Practices like mindfulness-based stress reduction (MBSR) and transcendental meditation (TM) train your brain to focus on the present moment, lowering stress reaction and encouraging relaxation. Apps like Headspace and Calm offer guided meditations specifically designed for reproductive support.

Calming Techniques: Deep breathing exercises, gradual muscular relaxation, and visualization techniques can stimulate the parasympathetic nervous system, increasing calm and counteracting the "fight-or-flight" reaction.

Yoga & Tai Chi: These easy yet effective practices integrate movement with breathwork and mindfulness, encouraging relaxation, developing body awareness, and decreasing stress hormones.

Cognitive Behavioral Therapy (CBT): This therapy helps identify and eliminate negative thought patterns that contribute to stress and anxiety, helping you to regulate emotions and negotiate problems efficiently.

Connecting with Nature: Immersing oneself in nature, whether it's a walk in the park or gardening, has been shown to reduce stress hormones and increase mood.

Creative Expression: Engaging in hobbies like journaling, art, music, or dancing allows you to express emotions in a healthy way and manage stress efficiently.

Social Support: Building a strong support network with friends, family, or therapy groups can provide emotional support, understanding, and a feeling of community during the fertility journey.

The Power of Consistency:

Stress management isn't a one-time remedy; it's an ongoing process. Finding strategies you enjoy and putting them into your everyday routine is crucial. Start small, experiment, and be patient. The cumulative effect of these behaviors will progressively optimize your stress response and provide a fertile environment for conception.

Additional Tips for Success:

Identify Stress causes: Recognizing what causes your stress reaction is vital for establishing effective coping techniques. Keep a stress diary to uncover patterns and triggers.

Time Management & Organization: Feeling overloaded can worsen stress. Implement time management skills and prioritize tasks to reduce stress and boost feelings of control.

Seek Professional Help: If managing stress becomes overwhelming or you're struggling to cope, don't hesitate to seek professional help from a therapist or counselor specialized in stress management or reproductive concerns.

Remember, Self-Care Isn't Selfish: Prioritizing your well-being isn't a luxury; it's necessary for both your physical and emotional health. Taking care of yourself sets the foundation for a healthy conception and a pleasurable pregnant journey.

By taking an active approach to stress management, you're not just enhancing your fertility potential, but investing in your general well-being and laying a foundation for a healthy and rewarding future. Remember, you are not alone on this path, and with the correct tools and assistance, you can realize your dream of parenthood.

3. Sleep and its Fertility-Boosting Magic:

When it comes to fertility, we often focus on food, exercise, and stress management. But there's another essential lifestyle aspect that often goes overlooked: sleep. Getting enough quality sleep is vital for overall health and well-being, but it also has an unexpected role in enhancing your chances of conception. Let's go deeper into how sleep affects fertility and examine techniques to reach that lovely slumber:
Sleep's Symphony of Hormones:
Our sleep-wake cycle, regulated by the circadian rhythm, orchestrates a delicate ballet of hormones needed for reproductive function:

Melatonin: Produced during darkness, melatonin regulates sleep and also interacts with reproductive hormones. In women, it supports egg quality and maturation. In men, it regulates testosterone production, crucial for sperm production and health.

Gonadotropin-releasing Hormone (GnRH): Released by the hypothalamus, GnRH stimulates the pituitary gland to release FSH and LH, which are necessary for ovulation and sperm production. Insufficient sleep alters GnRH secretion, harming both egg and sperm health.

Sex Hormones: Sleep deprivation can lead to abnormalities in estrogen, progesterone, and cortisol, further limiting ovulation and perhaps raising miscarriage risk.

The Impact of Sleep Deprivation:
Chronic sleep deprivation, defined as routinely getting less than 7 hours of sleep every night, might significantly influence fertility in various ways:

Reduced Egg Quality: In women, poor sleep can lead to irregular cycles, reduced ovarian reserve, and impaired egg development, reducing fertilization success.

Lower Sperm Quality: Men experiencing sleep deprivation generally demonstrate decreased sperm count, motility, and morphology, limiting their ability to reach and fertilize the egg.

Increased Stress: Sleep loss boosts stress hormones like cortisol, which further affects the hormonal balance necessary for conception.

Reduced Libido: Both men and women having sleep disorders may have lower sexual desire and intimacy, hampering conception efforts.

Sweet Dreams for Fertility Success: Fortunately, prioritizing sleep can dramatically boost your chances of conceiving:

Aim for 7-8 Hours: Most individuals need 7-8 hours of excellent sleep per night for optimal health and fertility. Consistency is crucial, striving for consistent sleep and waking hours even on weekends.

Create a Relaxing Sleep Environment: Ensure your bedroom is dark, quiet, cool, and free from distractions like technology. Invest in a comfy mattress and pillows.

Develop a Sleep ritual: Establish a peaceful
nighttime ritual that communicates to your body
it's time to wind down. Try taking a warm bath,
reading a book, or practicing mild stretches
before bed.

Limit coffee and Alcohol: Avoid coffee and alcohol
close to bedtime, as these can interfere with
sleep quality.

Regular Exercise: Engage in regular physical
activity, but avoid hard activities close to
bedtime.

Manage Stress: Implement stress management
strategies like meditation, yoga, or deep
breathing to relax your mind and prepare for
sleep.

Seek Professional Help: If you have problems
sleeping, visit a doctor to rule out underlying
sleep disorders and explore treatment
alternatives.

Remember:
Getting enough sleep isn't just about counting
sheep; it's about prioritizing your entire
well-being. By embracing proper sleep habits,
you're not just setting the basis for a restful

night, but also optimizing your hormone balance, strengthening your physical and mental health, and eventually increasing your chances of realizing your dream of parenting.

Additional Tips:
Limit Screen Time Before Bed: The blue light released from electronic gadgets can block melatonin production, making it difficult to fall asleep. Avoid screens for at least an hour before bedtime.

Create a Relaxing Evening Ritual: Develop a calming habit before bed, such as taking a warm bath, listening to soothing music, or reading a book.

Expose Yourself to sunshine: Get regular exposure to natural sunshine during the day to help regulate your circadian cycle and encourage healthier sleep at night.

Avoid large Meals Before Bed: Eating a large meal close to bedtime can impair sleep. Opt for a light, healthful snack if needed.

By implementing these sleep-promoting methods into your life, you're giving yourself the gift of great sleep and, in turn, establishing a fertile environment for conception and a healthy pregnancy journey.

Remember, prioritizing your sleep is an investment in your general well-being and opens the way to accomplishing your dream of parenthood.

Sleep and the Hormonal Orchestra:
Beyond the basic concept of sleep controlling melatonin, let's dive deeper into the complicated chemical symphony sleep directs for fertility:

Melatonin's Multifaceted Role: While melatonin indicates slumber, it also directly interacts with reproductive hormones:

Women: Melatonin supports the maturation of ovarian follicles, altering egg quality and perhaps delaying ovulation in women with PCOS.

Men: Melatonin receptors are present in testes, suggesting a role in regulating testosterone synthesis and sperm formation.

GnRH & the Pituitary Connection: Sleep deprivation disturbs the sensitive timing of GnRH release, which in turn impacts FSH and LH production. This hormonal cascade ultimately influences egg formation, maturation, and ovulation in women, and sperm production in men.

Sex Hormone Imbalance: Insufficient sleep leads to abnormalities in estrogen, progesterone, and cortisol:

Reduced Estrogen: Crucial for ovulation and implantation, insufficient estrogen due to sleep deprivation can alter the menstrual cycle and hamper pregnancy.

Progesterone Fluctuations: Sleep difficulties can create unpredictable progesterone levels, influencing the uterine lining growth and lowering implantation success.

Elevated Cortisol: Chronic stress produced by sleep loss boosts cortisol, further disturbing the delicate hormonal balance needed for conception.

Sleep Deprivation: A Chain Reaction for Fertility: Understanding the hormonal influence is simply one element of the problem. Let's study the downstream consequences of sleep loss on fertility:

DNA Damage: Insufficient sleep increases oxidative stress, leading to DNA damage in both eggs and sperm, reducing their health and fertilization ability.

Immune System Function: Sleep deprivation impairs the immune system, making both men and women more susceptible to illnesses that might impact reproductive health.

Inflammation: Sleep disorders induce chronic low-grade inflammation, producing an adverse environment for conception and implantation.

Reduced Sex Drive: Both men and women experiencing sleep loss generally report lower libido and less interest in intimacy, limiting conception efforts.

Unlocking Fertility with Sweet Dreams: By prioritizing sleep, you can greatly boost your chances of getting pregnant:

Optimize Sleep Duration: Aim for 7-9 hours of decent sleep per night. Consistency is crucial, maintaining a regular sleep-wake routine even on weekends.

Craft Your Sleep Sanctuary: Make your bedroom dark, quiet, cool, and clutter-free. Invest in a comfy mattress, pillows, and blackout curtains.

Wind Down with a Routine: Develop a calm nighttime routine that communicates to your body it's time to unwind. Consider warm baths, mild stretches, meditation, or reading a book.

Fuel Your Body Wisely: Limit coffee and alcohol, especially close to bedtime. Opt for light, healthful meals in the evening.

Move Your Body: Regular moderate activity improves deeper sleep, but avoid hard activities before bed.

Manage Stress: Implement stress management strategies like yoga, deep breathing, or spending time in nature to relax your mind and prepare for sleep.

Seek Professional Help: If you have chronic sleep disorders, visit a doctor or sleep specialist to rule out underlying conditions and explore treatment options.

Additional Tips for Sleep Success:
Embrace Sunlight: Regular exposure to natural light during the day helps regulate your circadian cycle and promotes healthier sleep at night.

Power Down Before Bed: Avoid screen time for at least an hour before sleep, as the blue light released decreases melatonin production.

Create a Relaxing Evening Ritual: Wind down with calming activities like taking a warm bath, listening to soothing music, or practicing mindfulness techniques.

Invest in Relaxation Techniques: Consider incorporating meditation, progressive muscle relaxation, or guided imagery into your evening routine.

Listen to Your Body: Don't push sleep; if you can't fall asleep after 20 minutes, get out of bed and undertake a calming activity until you feel drowsy.

Remember, sleep is not a luxury but a requirement for both your physical and mental wellbeing. By prioritizing sleep and adopting healthy sleep habits, you're taking control of your fertility journey and building a strong foundation for a safe pregnancy and a joyous future. So, embrace the power of sleep and unlock the door to realizing your dream of parenthood!

4. Avoiding Toxins: Avoiding Toxins: A Crucial Step for Enhancing Fertility

While often ignored, reducing exposure to environmental contaminants has a surprising yet essential role in optimizing fertility for both men and women. These toxins can hide in all elements of our daily lives, from the air we breathe to the food we eat, and can disrupt the delicate hormonal balance required for conception. Let's look into the specific concerns of toxins for fertility and investigate measures to limit their impact:

The Toxic Threat to Fertility:

Toxins can affect fertility in numerous ways:

Hormonal Disruption: Many chemicals are endocrine disruptors, mimicking or interfering with natural hormones including estrogen, progesterone, and testosterone. This disruption can impede egg development, ovulation, sperm production, and ultimately, fertilization success.

DNA Damage: Exposure to chemicals can directly damage the DNA in eggs and sperm, altering their health and limiting their ability to fertilize and develop into a healthy embryo.

Oxidative Stress: Toxins can generate an environment of oxidative stress, harming cells and inhibiting crucial reproductive functions.

Specific Toxins and their Fertility Impact:

Bisphenol A (BPA): Found in plastics, linings of canned products, and thermal receipts, BPA can mimic estrogen and affect ovarian function in women and sperm development in males.

Phthalates: Used in plastics, personal care items, and scents, phthalates can influence testosterone levels and sperm quality in males.
Heavy Metals: Lead, mercury, and arsenic can build in the body and impair both egg and sperm health.

Pesticides and Herbicides: Exposure to these agricultural pesticides can disturb hormonal balance and potentially influence sperm quality.

Air Pollution: Pollutants such fine particulate matter (PM2.5) can enter the circulation and reach reproductive organs, reducing egg quality and sperm health.

Strategies for Minimizing Toxin Exposure:

Fortunately, you may take control and decrease your exposure to hazardous toxins:

Eat Organic: Opting for organic fruits, vegetables, and meat decreases pesticide and herbicide residues.

Read Labels Carefully: Choose items made with BPA-free and phthalate-free plastics. Look for personal care products devoid of dangerous substances.

Invest in Water Filters: Filter your drinking water to remove toxins including lead, mercury, and chlorine.

Cook More at Home: Preparing meals from scratch helps you to manage the ingredients and avoid hidden contaminants in packaged foods.

Store Food Safely: Avoid storing food in plastic containers, especially when hot. Opt for glass or stainless steel containers.

Wash Thoroughly: Wash fruits and vegetables thoroughly to remove pesticide residues.

Ventilate Your Home: Regularly open windows and doors to increase air circulation and reduce indoor air pollution.

Use Natural Cleaning Products: Avoid harsh chemical cleaners and instead for natural, vinegar-based options.

Declutter Your Space: Minimizing clutter decreases dust formation, which can harbor pollutants.

Practice Good Hygiene: Wash your hands frequently to remove potential poisons from your environment.

Remember:

Focus on Progress, Not Perfection: Eliminating all pollutants is unrealistic. Focus on making incremental changes and reducing exposure where possible.
Consult Your Doctor: If you have concerns about certain chemicals or are undergoing fertility treatment, address them with your healthcare provider.

Beyond only enhancing fertility:

Reducing toxin exposure isn't just about conception; it's about addressing your complete health and well-being. By avoiding exposure to dangerous chemicals, you're creating a cleaner, healthier environment for yourself and your future family.

Additional Tips:

Support Detoxification: Encourage your body's natural detoxification processes by eating lots of fruits, vegetables, and fiber, drinking adequate water, and indulging in regular exercise.

Stay Informed: Research current information regarding hazardous toxins and their impact on fertility to make informed choices.

Advocate for Change: Support organizations working to eliminate environmental pollutants and promote safer products.

By embracing these tactics and making conscious decisions, you can empower yourself to minimize your exposure to toxins, optimize your reproductive potential, and pave the path for a healthy and enjoyable journey into parenting. Remember, you have the power to create a better future for yourself and your future family.

The Specific Mechanisms of Toxin Harm:

Let's study the intricate ways pollutants hinder fertility:

Endocrine Disruption: Many pollutants operate as endocrine disruptors, mimicking or interfering with key hormones including estrogen, progesterone, and testosterone. This interruption can:
Women: Disrupt ovarian function, influencing egg formation, maturation, and ovulation.

Men: Affect testosterone levels, sperm production, and motility.

DNA Damage: Toxins can directly damage the DNA in eggs and sperm, causing:

Chromosomal abnormalities: Leading to miscarriage or birth problems.

Reduced fertilization potential: Damaged DNA inhibits the capacity to fertilize or develop into a healthy embryo.

Oxidative Stress: Exposure to toxins causes an environment of oxidative stress, affecting cells in numerous ways:

Damages cell membranes: Essential for optimal egg and sperm development.

Reduces antioxidant levels: Crucial for neutralizing free radicals and safeguarding cells.

Increases inflammation: Disrupts delicate hormonal balance and inhibits reproductive function.
Beyond the Usual Suspects:

While BPA, phthalates, and heavy metals are generally known reproductive disruptors, numerous other chemicals warrant attention:

Flame Retardants: Found in furniture, electronics, and building materials, they can alter thyroid function and potentially impact hormone control.

Per- and Polyfluoroalkyl Substances (PFAS): Used in non-stick cookware, water-resistant clothing, and stain repellents, they can build in the body and potentially influence sperm quality and hormone levels.

Persistent Organic Pollutants (POPs): Found in pesticides, industrial waste, and some foods, they can build in the body and affect reproductive hormones.

Individualized Strategies for Minimizing Exposure:

While avoiding all pollutants is impractical, adjusting your strategy depending on your lifestyle and concerns can dramatically reduce exposure:
Dietary Choices:

Organic vs. Conventional: Opt for organic produce whenever possible, especially for items with high pesticide residues like leafy greens and berries.

Meat & Dairy Sources: Choose hormone-free and antibiotic-free meat and dairy products to avoid exposure to potential endocrine disruptors.

Cook More at Home: This helps you to manage ingredients and avoid hidden poisons in packaged foods.

Consider Plant-Based Options: Studies suggest plant-based diets may limit exposure to certain pollutants and give other health benefits.

Personal Care Products:

Read Labels Carefully: Opt for products free of parabens, phthalates, and other known endocrine disruptors. Look for certifications like "EWG Verified" or "USDA Organic."

Consider Natural options: Explore natural options like coconut oil for shaving or baking soda for deodorant.
Minimize Fragrance Exposure: Limit the use of perfumes, air fresheners, and scented candles, as they often contain dangerous compounds.

Household Products:

Natural Cleaning Solutions: Ditch harsh chemical cleaners and use natural alternatives like vinegar and baking soda.

Minimize Plastic Use: Avoid plastic containers, especially when hot, and go for glass or stainless steel alternatives.

Improve Ventilation: Regularly open windows and doors to reduce indoor air pollution.

Invest in Air Purifiers: Consider HEPA air purifiers to eliminate fine particulate matter (PM2.5) and other contaminants from your indoor air.

Remember:

Small adjustments Make a Difference: Focus on making modest adjustments that are sustainable in the long term.

Seek Professional Guidance: Consult your doctor or a fertility specialist for individualized guidance on limiting toxin exposure according to your needs and concerns.

Advocate for Change: Support organizations working to eliminate environmental pollutants and promote safer products.

By emphasizing healthy choices and reducing exposure to dangerous pollutants, you're not just enhancing your fertility, but also investing in your overall health and well-being. Remember, you have the power to create a better future for yourself and your future family.

Additional Tips:

Detoxification Support: While the body has natural detoxification pathways, consider combining techniques like liver support supplements or detoxifying diets under professional guidance.

Stay Informed: Follow trustworthy sources for information on emerging research and advice surrounding chemicals and fertility.

Connect with Others: Join online communities or support groups focused on limiting toxic exposure and enhancing fertility health. Remember, the route to motherhood is individual, and arming yourself with knowledge and taking action towards avoiding toxin exposure is a crucial step towards building a fruitful and healthy environment for conception and a joyous future.

Chapter Six:

Addressing Common Challenges

It's vital to remember that every individual's condition is unique, and seeking competent medical guidance is crucial for correct diagnosis and treatment. Discussing specific reproductive issues and treatment alternatives requires comprehensive examination and experience from a doctor or specialist familiar with your unique circumstances.

Here's a breakdown of some frequent issues in fertility for conception:

Common Female Factors:

Ovulation disorders: This includes problems like Polycystic Ovary Syndrome (PCOS) and irregular menstrual periods that can limit egg release.

Fallopian tube issues: Blockages or damage to the fallopian tubes might delay sperm and egg from meeting.

Endometriosis: Tissue comparable to the uterine lining grows outside the uterus, potentially hindering implantation.

Uterine abnormalities: Fibroids, polyps, or structural difficulties might produce an inappropriate environment for conception.

Age: Fertility naturally falls with age, especially for women in their late 30s and 40s.

Common Male Factors:

Low sperm count or motility: Reduced sperm number or weak mobility might make fertilization difficult.

Abnormal sperm morphology: Sperm shape abnormalities can hamper their ability to reach and fertilize the egg.

Undescended testicles: Untreated childhood disorders might decrease sperm production.

Hormonal imbalances: Low testosterone levels can impair sperm production and function.

Varicocele: Enlarged veins in the scrotum can boost testicular temperature, affecting sperm health.

Lifestyle factors:

Weight: Both underweight and obesity can significantly affect fertility in both men and women.

Diet: Poor diet might impact hormone balance and sperm quality.

Smoking and alcohol: These practices can impair sperm health and egg quality.

Stress: Chronic stress can impair hormone balance and ovulation.

Environmental toxins: Exposure to some substances can damage sperm and egg production.

Addressing these challenges:

Seek professional help: Consult a doctor or fertility specialist for diagnosis, personalized treatment options, and emotional support.

Consider lifestyle changes: Maintaining a healthy weight, eating a balanced diet, minimizing stress, and avoiding dangerous substances can dramatically boost fertility.

Explore therapy options: Depending on the precise cause, numerous treatments are available, including fertility medicines, surgery, assisted reproductive technologies like IVF, and alternative therapies.

Note:
This is just a general overview, and getting competent medical guidance is vital for proper diagnosis and individualized treatment regimens.

There are various services available to support people and couples with fertility issues, such as national fertility organizations, local support groups, and internet forums.

Be patient and understanding. Fertility treatments might take time and may not always be successful.

1. Low Sperm Count:

Low sperm count, medically known as oligospermia, is a primary factor contributing to male infertility and poses a substantial obstacle for couples trying to conceive. Here's a thorough breakdown of its impact on fertility and conception:

The Numbers Game:

Definition: A sperm count is deemed poor if it goes below 15 million sperm per milliliter (mL) of semen, according to the World Health Organization (WHO). The usual healthy count is roughly 39 million/mL.

Impact on Fertility: Even with reduced numbers, conception is still feasible naturally, but chances decrease dramatically. Studies reveal males with counts below 10 million/mL have a reduced risk of conception compared to those with higher counts.

Causes and Risk Factors:

Lifestyle: Smoking, excessive alcohol use, recreational drug use, and obesity can all significantly affect sperm production.

Medical Conditions: Underlying health conditions including varicocele (enlarged veins in the scrotum), undescended testicles, infections like mumps or HIV, and hormonal imbalances (low testosterone) can contribute.

Environmental Factors: Exposure to some chemicals, herbicides, and heavy metals has been associated with lower sperm counts.

Genetic Factors: Chromosomal abnormalities and hereditary diseases can have a role.

Diagnosis and Evaluation:

Semen Analysis: This simple test analyzes sperm concentration, motility (movement), and morphology (shape). Multiple analyses throughout time may be needed for appropriate diagnosis.

Hormonal Testing: Blood tests evaluate testosterone and other hormones potentially affecting sperm development.

Imaging Tests: Ultrasound or testicular biopsy may be utilized to explore particular problems like varicocele.

Treatment Options:

Lifestyle Modifications: Addressing contributory lifestyle factors like food, exercise, and substance usage might be useful.

Medicines: Depending on the cause, hormonal medicines or treatments addressing underlying medical issues may boost sperm production.

Assisted Reproductive Technologies (ART): If natural conception remains problematic, several ART treatments including intrauterine insemination (IUI) or in vitro fertilization (IVF) can be considered.

Additional Considerations:

Emotional Impact: Facing infertility can be emotionally hard, and getting help from spouses, therapists, or support groups can be valuable.

Prognosis: The outcome of treatment relies on the severity and reason of the low sperm count. Early diagnosis and intervention can dramatically improve the odds of achieving pregnancy.

Research and Advances: Research into the causes and treatment of low sperm count is ongoing, bringing hope for future improvements in diagnosis and management.

Remember:

While low sperm count is a typical difficulty, it doesn't inevitably indicate conception is impossible.

Seeking professional medical advice and pursuing proper treatment options are vital for optimizing reproductive potential.

Maintaining a healthy lifestyle and managing stress can further boost general well-being during the reproductive process.

Let's study particular aspects further:

Sperm Quality: While focusing on count is vital, remember "quality" comprises multiple factors:

Motility: Do sperm migrate efficiently to reach the egg? Poor motility (asthenozoospermia) drastically lowers the possibility of fertilization.

Morphology: Are sperm shaped normally? Abnormal shapes (teratozoospermia) can impede their capacity to penetrate the egg.

Vitality: Are sperm alive and functioning well? Dead or inactive sperm cannot fertilize an egg.

Understanding Specific Causes:

Varicocele: This is the most prevalent reason, affecting around 15% of males with low sperm count. Enlarged veins in the scrotum raise testicular warmth, impacting sperm production. Treatment involves minimally invasive surgery to mend the veins.

Hormonal Imbalances: Low testosterone is a typical cause, often linked to other health issues including obesity or genetic reasons. Hormone replacement therapy can repair inadequacies and boost sperm production.

Genetic Factors: Genetic disorders, including Klinefelter syndrome, can impact sperm production. Genetic testing may be recommended if other explanations are ruled out. Infection and Inflammation: Testicular infections or inflammation can destroy sperm-producing cells. Prompt detection and treatment of underlying infections are critical.

Environmental Exposures: Exposure to some chemicals, insecticides, and heavy metals can significantly affect sperm health. Minimizing exposure and establishing healthy lifestyle practices are key.

Treatment Options in Detail:

Lifestyle Modifications: Maintaining a healthy weight, eating a balanced diet rich in antioxidants and important nutrients (zinc, folate, vitamin D), frequent exercise, and stress management can greatly improve sperm quality and count.

Drugs: Depending on the exact cause, drugs such antibiotics for infections, hormone therapy for deficiencies, or medications to increase sperm motility might be administered.

Surgical Interventions: Varicocele repair surgery is a frequent surgical method to enhance sperm production. Other procedures can be necessary in specific instances, like repairing obstructions in the reproductive tract.

Alternative and Complementary Therapies: While data is limited, several studies show acupuncture, yoga, and certain supplements might offer some benefits for sperm health. However, consult a healthcare expert before using any supplement, as interactions with drugs can arise.

Advanced Techniques and Emerging Research:

Intracytoplasmic Sperm Injection (ICSI): This modern ART procedure injects a single healthy sperm directly into the egg, bypassing motility and morphological concerns.

Sperm retrieval techniques: In cases of severe low sperm count or blockages, surgical sperm retrieval methods such testicular sperm extraction (TESE) are utilized to retrieve sperm for ICSI.

Stem cell research: Ongoing study explores the prospect of utilizing stem cells to create sperm cells, presenting promise for future treatment options.

Note:
This material is meant for general understanding only and should not be regarded as a substitute for professional medical advice. Always consult a healthcare professional for specialized diagnosis and treatment of reproductive difficulties.

2. Cervical Mucus Issues: A Sticky Situation in Fertility

While not as often publicized as other fertility obstacles, cervical mucus issues can indeed play a part in conception difficulties. Let's look deeper into this potential obstacle:

The Role of Cervical Mucus:

This naturally produced cervical discharge serves two critical functions:

Barrier: During non-fertile phases, it works as a barrier, filtering out microorganisms and preventing sperm from accessing the uterus.

Highway: During ovulation, it turns into a fertile, clear, stretchy "egg white cervical mucus (EWCM)" that aids sperm passage towards the egg.

Types of Cervical Mucus Issues:

Scant or Absent Mucus: This might inhibit sperm motility, making their travel to the egg more arduous. Causes include hormone imbalances, stress, certain drugs, or underlying health concerns.

Hostile Mucus: Sometimes, the mucus is acidic or contains antibodies that target and kill sperm. This can arise owing to infections, allergies, or autoimmune diseases.

Cervical stenosis: A constricted or closed cervix can physically block sperm flow. This might be caused by scar tissue after surgery, childbirth, or infections.

Impact on Fertility:

If the mucus fails to offer a favorable environment for sperm survival and motility, conception becomes less likely. However, it's crucial to realize that cervical mucous difficulties are rarely the single cause of infertility and often occur alongside other contributing factors.

Diagnosis and Evaluation:

Pelvic Exam: A healthcare practitioner can check the cervix and mucus consistency and quantity.

Ovulation Tracking: Monitoring cervical mucus variations during your cycle can identify potential concerns.

Hormonal Testing: Blood tests could be done to look for hormonal imbalances that could alter mucus production.

Cervical cultures: These tests screen for illnesses that can be contributing to unfriendly mucus.

Treatment Options:

Addressing Underlying Causes: Treating any underlying issues including infections, hormonal imbalances, or allergies will improve mucus quality.

Lifestyle Modifications: Maintaining a healthy weight, reducing stress, and avoiding smoking can indirectly benefit cervical mucus production.

Cervical dilation techniques: In rare situations, a healthcare professional could use a catheter to temporarily open the cervix and promote sperm passage.

Additional Considerations:

Individual Variations: Cervical mucus naturally varies in consistency and volume among individuals and across cycles. Not getting EWCM every month doesn't inherently imply a problem.

Seeking Professional Help: If you feel cervical mucus difficulties might be harming your fertility, visit a healthcare professional for diagnosis and appropriate management techniques.

Emotional Support: Facing fertility issues can be emotionally challenging. Seeking support groups, therapy, or open communication with partners might be beneficial.

Remember:

This information is meant for general understanding and should not be regarded as a substitute for professional medical advice.

Cervical mucous difficulties are just one potential contributor in reproductive challenges.

Early identification and addressing underlying reasons are critical for optimal reproductive potential.

Let's study particular aspects further:

Understanding Hostile Mucus:

Causes: Beyond infections, allergies, and autoimmune diseases, other causes can contribute to hostile mucus:

Diet: Processed meals, excessive sugar, and caffeine intake can severely affect cervical health and mucus quality.

Lubricants: Using some non-sperm-friendly lubricants during intercourse can interfere with sperm mobility and survival in the mucus.

Douches: Douching alters the natural vaginal environment, potentially affecting the composition and pH of cervical mucus.

Stress: Chronic stress can boost cortisol levels, disrupting hormonal balance and perhaps affecting mucus production.

Diagnostic Techniques:

Postcoital Test (PCT): This test examines sperm survival and migration throughout the cervical mucus following intercourse. However, its interpretation can be subjective and is not necessarily definitive.

Hysterosalpingography (HSG): This X-ray examination with contrast dye examines for obstructions in the fallopian tubes and can indirectly measure the cervix and mucus flow.

Endometrial biopsy: In rare circumstances, a tissue sample from the uterine lining could be evaluated for evidence of inflammation or hormonal abnormalities impacting mucus production.

Treatment Options in Detail:

Dietary Modifications: Prioritizing whole meals, fruits, vegetables, and healthy fats can maintain hormonal balance and potentially improve cervical health.

Sperm-friendly Lubricants: Opting for water-based or lubricants specifically made for fertility can create a more hospitable environment for sperm.

Avoiding Douching: Douching is unnecessary and can be damaging to vaginal health. Opt for gentle cleansing with water only.

Stress Management Techniques: Practices like yoga, meditation, and deep breathing can help control stress levels and potentially enhance cervical mucus quality.

Antibiotics or Antifungal Medications: If infections are discovered, specific medications will be provided to tackle the underlying cause.

Antihistamines: For allergy-related disorders, antihistamines could be advised to reduce inflammation and improve mucus composition.

Hormonal Medications: In cases of hormonal imbalances affecting mucus production, hormone therapy could be administered.

Emerging Research and Future Directions:

Studies are studying the possibility of probiotics and vaginal suppositories to restore a healthy vaginal microbiome and enhance cervical mucus quality.

Research is ongoing to understand the complicated interplay between lifestyle variables, food, and the vaginal microbiome's impact on cervical mucus and fertility.

Remember:
This information is still for general understanding and does not replace expert medical advice.

Individual experiences and reasons for cervical mucous difficulties might vary substantially.

Consulting a healthcare professional for tailored diagnosis and treatment is vital.

Emotional support and open communication with partners and healthcare providers are vital throughout the fertility journey.

3. Other Medical Conditions:

While we've dug into low sperm count and cervical mucus concerns, various additional medical illnesses might cause challenges for conception. Here's a closer look at some typical culprits:

Female-Specific Conditions:

Endometriosis: Tissue identical to the uterine lining grows outside the uterus, producing inflammation, discomfort, and possible scarring, hindering egg implantation.

Polycystic ovarian syndrome (PCOS): Hormonal imbalances impair ovulation, resulting in irregular periods, numerous cysts in ovaries, and perhaps diminished egg quality.

Pelvic inflammatory disease (PID): Untreated sexually transmitted infections can cause scarring in the fallopian tubes, impeding egg transport and fertilization.

Uterine fibroids: Non-cancerous growths in the uterus can restrict fallopian tubes or impede with implantation.

Premature ovarian failure (POF): Ovaries stop functioning prematurely, leading to decreased egg production and earlier menopause.

Thyroid disorders: Both hyperactive and underactive thyroid glands can impair ovulation and hormone control.

Male-Specific Conditions:

Undescended testicles: If testicles don't descend into the scrotum during development, sperm production can be limited.

Varicocele: Enlarged veins around the testicles boost temperature, potentially reducing sperm quality and production.

Retrograde ejaculation: Semen travels backward into the bladder instead of being ejected externally during orgasm.

Erectile dysfunction and premature ejaculation: These difficulties can make obtaining or maintaining an erection or ejaculating sperm within the vagina problematic.

Shared Conditions:

Celiac disease: An autoimmune illness produced by gluten can disrupt nutritional absorption and impact hormone balance, potentially compromising both male and female fertility.

Diabetes: Uncontrolled blood sugar levels can impair ovulation, sperm quality, and general reproductive health in both genders.

Obesity and being underweight: Both extremes can impact hormone control and ovulation in women and sperm production in males.

Certain drugs: Some treatments, including chemotherapy, can temporarily or permanently impair fertility in both men and women.

Remember:
This list is not exhaustive, as many other medical disorders can impair fertility.

Early detection and management of any underlying medical condition can dramatically boost reproductive potential.

Seeking skilled medical guidance for tailored diagnosis and treatment is vital.

Open communication with partners and healthcare providers can provide support and direction throughout the fertility journey.

It's crucial to note that each illness has its own peculiarities, and individual experiences might differ substantially. Consulting a healthcare professional for tailored diagnosis and treatment is vital.

Focusing on Specific Conditions:

1. Endometriosis:

Details: Tissue identical to the uterine lining grows outside the uterus, producing inflammation, discomfort, and scarring. This can impact egg implantation and fallopian tube function.

Diagnosis: Laparoscopy is the gold standard, however pelvic ultrasonography and MRI can also be performed.

Treatment: Hormone therapy, pain management, and surgery for severe instances.

2. Polycystic Ovary Syndrome (PCOS):

Details: Hormonal imbalances interrupt ovulation, leading to irregular periods, numerous cysts in ovaries, and potentially lower egg quality.

Diagnosis: Blood tests and ultrasound.

Treatment: Lifestyle adjustments (diet, exercise), medicines to regulate ovulation, and fertility therapies like IUI or IVF.

3. Pelvic Inflammatory Disease (PID):

Details: Untreated sexually transmitted infections (STIs) can induce scarring in the fallopian tubes, impeding egg transport and fertilization.

Diagnosis: Pelvic exam, swabs for STI testing, and sometimes ultrasound.

Treatment: Antibiotics for the STI, pain treatment, and surgery for severe instances.

4. Uterine Fibroids:

Details: Non-cancerous growths in the uterus might restrict fallopian tubes or impede with implantation.

Diagnosis: Pelvic exam, ultrasound, or MRI.

Treatment: Monitoring, medication to reduce fibroids, or surgery depending on size and location.

5. Premature Ovarian Failure (POF):

Details: Ovaries stop functioning prematurely, leading to decreased egg production and earlier menopause.

Diagnosis: Blood testing for hormone levels.

Treatment: Hormone therapy to moderate symptoms, egg freezing for future use, and fertility therapies like donor eggs or adoption.

6. Undescended Testicles:

Details: If testicles don't descend into the scrotum during development, sperm production can be limited.

Diagnosis: Physical exam.

Treatment: Surgery to relocate the testicles into the scrotum.

7. Varicocele:

Details: Enlarged veins around the testicles boost temperature, potentially reducing sperm quality and production.

Diagnosis: Physical exam and sometimes ultrasonography.

Treatment: Embolization or surgery to correct the swollen veins.

8. Retrograde Ejaculation:

Details: Semen moves backward into the bladder instead of being expelled externally after orgasm.

Diagnosis: Semen analysis and specific testing to confirm retrograde ejaculation.

Treatment: Medications to seal the bladder neck during ejaculation or sperm retrieval techniques for assisted reproductive technologies (ART).

Remember:

This information is still for general understanding and does not replace expert medical advice.

Early detection and management of any underlying medical condition can dramatically boost reproductive potential.

Seeking skilled medical guidance for tailored diagnosis and treatment is vital.

Open communication with partners and healthcare providers can provide support and direction throughout the fertility journey.

Chapter Seven:

Maintaining a Healthy Pregnancy: Cultivating Joy and Wellness

Pregnancy, a journey filled with expectation, excitement, and sometimes, a dash of dread, is a beautiful period of great transformation. As life begins to develop within you, keeping a healthy environment for your growing baby becomes important. This essay seeks to educate you through crucial aspects of sustaining a healthy pregnancy, empowering you to make informed decisions and enjoy this transformational journey with confidence.

Nurturing Your Body:

Eat Well, Be Well: Embark on a gastronomic excursion filled with a rainbow of fruits and vegetables, lean protein sources, entire grains, and healthy fats. Don't forget to stay hydrated – water is your best buddy! Prenatal vitamins, suggested by your healthcare professional, fill nutritional gaps. Remember, moderation is crucial, indulge in cravings periodically, but prefer healthier alternatives.

Move Your Body, Feel Empowered: Regular physical activity, customized to your needs and approved by your doctor, is a gift to your body and mind. Walking, swimming, pregnant yoga, or modified versions of your favorite exercises keep you energized, improve sleep, and manage pregnancy discomforts. Listen to your body, rest when needed, and enjoy the action.

Sleep, the Sweet Elixir: As your body works overtime, prioritize quality sleep. Aim for 7-8 hours each night, build a calm bedtime ritual, and generate a comfortable sleep environment. Adequate sleep fuels your energy, enhances immunity, and promotes both your and your baby's well-being.

Safeguarding Your Health:

Prenatal Care: Your Lifeline: Regular prenatal checks with your healthcare practitioner are vital. These visits check your health, resolve concerns, and provide helpful guidance. Ask inquiries, communicate your apprehensions, and create a trustworthy relationship with your healthcare staff.

Mindful Choices: Eliminate dangerous substances including alcohol, tobacco, and illegal drugs.

These pose major threats to your baby's growth. Be cautious with certain drugs and herbal supplements, always visiting your doctor before taking anything new.

Manage Existing disorders: If you have pre-existing medical disorders like diabetes or high blood pressure, diligent management is vital. Work together with your healthcare professional to promote optimal control and minimize pregnancy problems.

Emotional Well-being: The Unspoken Pillar:

Embrace the Emotional Rollercoaster: Pregnancy is an emotional whirlwind. Acknowledge your sensations, allow yourself to experience joy, worry, or even terror. Talk to loved ones, join support groups, or seek professional counseling if needed. Remember, you are not alone on this path.

Reduce Stress, Cultivate Calm: Chronic stress can harm your health and your baby's development. Practice relaxation techniques like deep breathing, meditation, or mindfulness exercises. Spend time in nature, engage in things you enjoy, and prioritize self-care.

Build a Strong Support System: Surround yourself with loving and supporting relatives and friends. Their encouragement, understanding, and practical help will be vital. Don't hesitate to ask for assistance, delegate responsibilities, and embrace the connections that boost you.

Note:

Every pregnancy is unique. Listen to your body, trust your instincts, and speak honestly with your healthcare professional. This path is yours to embrace, loaded with trials and immense rewards. Make informed choices, enjoy the milestones, and nurture both your physical and emotional well-being. With education, mindfulness, and self-care, you may develop a healthy pregnancy, laying the way for a pleasant and empowering experience.

Here's an exploration of several significant areas:

Nutrition:

Specific dietary groups: Focus on fruits, vegetables, whole grains, lean protein, and healthy fats. Include calcium-rich meals like dairy, leafy greens, and fortified alternatives for strong bones. Opt for iron-rich sources like red meat, lentils, and beans to prevent anemia.

Don't overlook vital vitamins like folic acid from fortified cereals, citrus fruits, and legumes, crucial for embryonic growth.

Hydration: Aim for 8-10 glasses of water daily to stay hydrated, help digestion, and reduce constipation, a major pregnancy worry. Consider herbal teas or fruit-infused water for variation.

Foods to limit: Minimize processed foods, sugary drinks, and excessive saturated and harmful fats. Limit caffeine intake as it can interfere with iron absorption. Avoid raw or undercooked meat, seafood, and eggs owing to potential bacterial hazards. Unpasteurized dairy products and some soft cheeses might house dangerous bacteria as well.

Exercise:

Safe and effective activities: Choose moderate-intensity workouts you enjoy, such brisk walking, swimming, prenatal yoga, or modified versions of your typical regimen. Aim for at least 150 minutes per week, but listen to your body and alter intensity as needed.

Precautions: Consult your doctor before starting any new exercise regimen, especially if you have pre-existing ailments. Avoid activities with a high risk of falling or contact sports. Modify exercises to avoid joint strain and overheating.

Benefits: Exercise improves mood, decreases stress, boosts energy, and promotes better sleep. It also helps manage weight growth, enhance circulation, and prepare your body for childbirth.

Prenatal Care:

Schedule and frequency: Regular prenatal checks are necessary. The frequency may vary depending on your trimester and individual demands. Discuss the schedule with your doctor.

What to expect: At checkups, your doctor will monitor your weight, blood pressure, fetal growth, and development through various tests. They will also address any issues and answer your questions.

Importance: Prenatal care helps identify and handle potential issues early, ensuring the best possible outcome for you and your baby.

Additional Considerations:

Mental health: Pregnancy can be emotionally demanding. Don't hesitate to seek support from therapists or counselors specializing in perinatal mental health.

Dental health: Good oral hygiene is vital throughout pregnancy. Regular dental checkups and thorough brushing/flossing are crucial.

Travel: Consult your doctor before traveling, especially overseas. Certain immunizations may be suggested, and particular destinations can offer dangers.

Community resources: Explore local prenatal support groups, birthing education classes, or lactation consultants for further assistance and connection.

Here are some extra research and expansions on critical areas to ensure a healthy pregnancy:

Sleep and Relaxation:

Importance of quality sleep: Adequate sleep (7-8 hours each night) is vital for your physical and mental well-being. It supports your immune system, energy levels, and emotional balance.

Lack of sleep can contribute to stress, worry, and exhaustion.

Tips for better sleep: Establish a regular sleep schedule, build a peaceful bedtime routine, ensure a comfortable sleep environment (cool temperature, darkness, quiet), and avoid computer time before bed. Consider relaxation techniques like deep breathing or meditation to wind down.

Managing common sleep disruptions: Pregnancy discomforts like indigestion, backache, or frequent urination can disrupt sleep. Use pillows for support, elevate your head while sleeping, and control symptoms with doctor-approved medications.

Stress Management:

Impact of stress on pregnancy: Chronic stress can raise the risk of problems like preterm birth and low birth weight. It can also influence your emotional well-being and parenting skills.

Healthy stress management techniques: Engage in things you enjoy like exercise, meditation, yoga, spending time in nature, listening to peaceful music, or connecting with loved ones.

Consider relaxing techniques like deep breathing, mindfulness exercises, or journaling.

Seeking expert help: If stress gets overwhelming, don't hesitate to seek professional help from therapists or counselors specialized in stress management or perinatal mental health.

Relationships and Support Systems:

Building a solid support network: Surround yourself with loving and supporting relatives and friends. Their encouragement, understanding, and practical aid can be vital. Consider joining pregnancy support groups or connecting with online communities for shared experiences and emotional support.

Communication with your partner: Open and honest communication with your partner is vital during pregnancy. Discuss your wants, anxieties, and expectations frankly. Share in household chores and obligations, and make choices jointly.

Preparing for parenthood: Consider attending childbirth education classes or workshops to learn about labor, delivery, and newborn care. Discussing parenting styles and expectations with your partner can also assist prepare for the move.

Additional Areas:

Skincare and body changes: Embrace the changes your body undergoes during pregnancy. Use mild, fragrance-free skincare products and moisturize regularly to manage stretch marks and dryness. Consult your doctor for any pregnancy-specific skin issues.

Sexual health: Discuss intimacy and sexual activity with your doctor, especially if you have any concerns or changes in your desire.

Financial planning: Consider the financial ramifications of having a kid and build a budget accordingly. Explore childcare choices, insurance needs, and government help programs if relevant.

Here's a further exploration of some significant areas:

Preparing for Labor and Delivery:

Birth plans: Create a birth plan including your choices for pain management, labor positions, interventions, and postpartum care. Remember, this is a fluid guide, and your needs may alter during childbirth.

Childbirth education: Consider attending childbirth education classes or seminars to learn about different birthing options, stages of labor, pain management strategies, and infant care. This can help you feel empowered and knowledgeable during delivery.

Discussing alternatives with your doctor: Talk to your doctor about your birthing preferences, concerns, and any potential danger factors. Discuss pain management alternatives like epidurals, different birth positions, and treatments you might be open to.

Postpartum Recovery and Care:

Physical recovery: Expect changes in your body after childbirth. Allow yourself time to recuperate and rest. Listen to your body and gradually return to physical exercise as directed by your doctor.

Emotional well-being: Postpartum sadness and anxiety are prevalent. Be aware of the signs and symptoms, and call out for help if needed. Seek support from family, friends, therapists, or support groups.

infant care: Learn about breastfeeding, bottle-feeding, swaddling, sleep habits, and infant needs. Attend newborn care seminars or visit with lactation specialists for more guidance.

Additional Areas:

Workplace accommodations: If you're working during your pregnancy, discuss essential accommodations with your employer to maintain a safe and comfortable work environment. This might include modifications to your tasks, breaks for pumping or feeding, or ergonomic adjustments.

Legal rights and resources: Familiarize yourself with your legal rights as a pregnant and postpartum person. Explore resources like maternity leave policies, health insurance coverage, and government assistance programs that might be available to you.

Environmental considerations: Minimize exposure to harmful environmental toxins during pregnancy and postpartum. Choose safe cleaning products, avoid second-hand smoke, and be mindful of potential risks in your home and work environment.

Remember:

Remember, these are general guidelines, and individual needs may vary. Always consult your healthcare provider for personalized advice and address any specific concerns you might have.

You are not alone! There are numerous resources and support systems available to help you navigate pregnancy and motherhood. Reach out and connect with others who can offer understanding, guidance, and emotional support.

1. Early Pregnancy Symptoms and What to Expect

The very early stages of pregnancy, about the first trimester, can be filled with joy, anticipation, and sometimes, uncertainty. While every woman's experience is unique, there are some common early pregnancy symptoms and things to expect:

Physical Symptoms:

Missed period: This is frequently the earliest and most telltale indicator of pregnancy, although not every missed period signifies pregnancy.

Breast changes: Tenderness, swelling, and darkening of the areolas are frequent.

Fatigue: Feeling abnormally weary is a common early symptom, related to hormonal changes.

Nausea and vomiting (morning sickness): This can occur at any time of day and affect women differently.

Frequent urination: Increased need to urinate due to changes in renal function and the expanding uterus.

Bloating and constipation: Hormonal changes and the digestive system slowing down might cause these concerns.

Light spotting or implantation bleeding: Some women experience spotting around the time of implantation, which is different from a usual period.

Food cravings and aversions: Changes in taste and scent can lead to significant preferences or dislikes for certain foods.

Emotional Symptoms:

Mood swings: Fluctuations in emotions are normal owing to hormonal fluctuations.

Irritability and anxiety: Feeling overwhelmed or on edge is understandable during this adjustment.

Increased emotional sensitivity: You might find yourself sobbing more easily or feeling more intensely.

What to Expect:

Prenatal appointments: Schedule your first prenatal appointment with your doctor or midwife as soon as you suspect you're pregnant. Regular checks guarantee your and your baby's health are closely checked.

Testing: Your doctor can recommend blood tests and ultrasounds to confirm pregnancy, examine your health, and track your baby's progress.

Lifestyle changes: Adjusting your nutrition, exercise regimen, and habits (such as stopping smoking) are vital for supporting a healthy pregnancy.

Prenatal vitamins: These give important nutrients you and your baby need.

Education: Take childbirth education programs or read widely to understand the birthing process and prepare for parenthood.

Building a support system: Surround yourself with caring and supportive relatives and friends who can offer emotional and practical assistance.

Important Notes:

Not every woman experiences all these symptoms: Some women could have few or no visible symptoms, while others experience a greater range.

The level of symptoms varies: Symptoms can be moderate or severe, and they might alter throughout the first trimester.

Consult your doctor for any concerns: Don't hesitate to contact your healthcare professional if you have any questions, concerns, or experience strange symptoms.

Embrace the journey: Remember, every pregnancy is unique and deserves to be cherished. Focus on keeping happy, informed, and supported as you embark on this great journey.

Building on the preceding material, here's a summary of early pregnancy symptoms with more data and specifics:

Missed Period:

Not experiencing your usual period is a major signal of pregnancy, although not necessarily certain. Stress, illness, or hormonal imbalances can also cause missing periods.

If you have a regular cycle and miss your period, consider taking a home pregnancy test, especially if you feel you could be pregnant. Most tests are accurate 7-10 days after ovulation.

Early discovery allows for earlier prenatal care, resulting in better pregnancy outcomes.

Breast Changes:

Tenderness, swelling, and tingling feelings in the breasts are frequent owing to increased blood flow and hormonal changes.

The areolas, the darker circles around the nipples, may start to darken and grow.

Montgomery glands, small lumps surrounding the areolas, could grow more noticeable.

Wearing a supportive and comfy bra might help decrease discomfort.

Fatigue:

Feeling abnormally weary is a common early symptom, often starting around week 4-6. It's caused by hormonal shifts, mainly progesterone, which promotes sleep but also makes you feel drowsy.

Getting enough rest is vital, but don't ignore mild exercise like walking or swimming, which can enhance energy levels.

Nausea and Vomiting (Morning Sickness):

Contrary to its name, this can occur at any time of day and varies significantly in intensity. It normally starts around week 4-6 and peaks around week 9-10, diminishing by week 13-14 for most women.

Certain triggers like harsh scents, fatty foods, or hunger might aggravate nausea. Eating small, regular meals, staying hydrated, and ginger can help alleviate symptoms.

Consult your doctor if vomiting is severe or interferes with everyday activities, as they can offer medication or other therapies.

Frequent Urination:

Increased need to urinate, especially at night, is frequent due to the developing uterus placing pressure on your bladder and hormonal changes altering kidney function.

Staying hydrated helps dilute urine and lessen discomfort. Empty your bladder fully wherever you go, and visit your doctor if you experience burning or pain while urinating, as it could suggest an infection.

Bloating and Constipation:

Hormonal fluctuations slow down digestion, leading to bloating and constipation.

Eating smaller, more often meals, boosting fiber intake, and drinking plenty of water will help ease these symptoms.

Gentle exercise might also assist digestion. Consult your doctor if constipation is severe or persistent.

Light Spotting or Implantation Bleeding:

Some women experience minor spotting or bleeding around the time of implantation (when the fertilized egg adheres to the uterine lining), usually 6-12 days following ovulation.

This is distinct from a regular period as the flow is often lighter and shorter.

If you have any bleeding during pregnancy, call your doctor to rule out any potential causes.

Food Cravings and Aversions:

Changes in taste and smell can lead to acute appetites for some meals or extreme aversions to others.

These are likely attributable to hormonal fluctuations and individual sensitivities.

Indulge in desires periodically, but prioritize a balanced diet rich in fruits, vegetables, healthy grains, and lean protein.

Remember, this information is for general awareness and should not be regarded as medical advice. Always consult your healthcare practitioner for tailored advice and address any unique concerns you might have.

By learning the early signs and symptoms of pregnancy, you can be well-prepared for this exciting and transforming time. Remember, information and open conversation with your healthcare practitioner are crucial to maintaining a healthy and enjoyable pregnant experience.

2. Prenatal Care and Healthy Habits

Congratulations on your pregnancy! Embarking on this journey demands informed choices and adopting healthy routines to give the best possible environment for your growing baby.
Let's go deep into two essential aspects: prenatal care and healthy habits:
Prenatal Care:

What it is: Regular checks with your healthcare provider (doctor, midwife) during your pregnancy to monitor your health, track your baby's progress, and treat any problems.

Frequency: Typically starts monthly in the first trimester, increasing to every other week in the second, and reaching weekly in the third trimester. Frequency might alter according to individual needs.

What happens during appointments:
Physical exams: Blood pressure, weight, and other vital signs are monitored. Abdominal exams assess your baby's growth and posture.

Tests: Blood tests screen for various conditions, and ultrasounds evaluate your baby's development.

Discussions: Concerns, symptoms, lifestyle choices, forthcoming testing, and delivery preferences are discussed.

Benefits: Early detection and control of any problems.

Education and knowledge about good pregnancy habits.

Emotional assistance and reassurance.

Building a trustworthy relationship with your healthcare provider.

Healthy Habits:

Diet: Aim for a balanced, nutrient-rich diet with plenty of fruits, vegetables, whole grains, lean protein, and healthy fats. Consume enough folic acid (via prenatal supplements or fortified meals) from early pregnancy to prevent birth abnormalities. Limit processed foods, sugary drinks, and excessive harmful fats. Stay hydrated with water throughout the day.

Exercise: Engage in moderate-intensity exercises like walking, swimming, or prenatal yoga, aiming for at least 150 minutes each week. Listen to your body, avoid high-impact exercises, and clear any new activities with your doctor. Exercise increases physical and mental well-being, helps regulate weight growth, and prepares your body for childbirth.

Sleep: Adequate sleep (7-8 hours each night) is vital for physical and mental wellness. Establish a consistent sleep schedule, build a pleasant nighttime routine, and prioritize sleep hygiene measures.

Stress management: Chronic stress can influence your health and your baby's development. Practice relaxation techniques like deep breathing, meditation, or yoga. Connect with loved ones, seek support groups, or consider therapy if needed.

Substance avoidance: Eliminate alcohol, tobacco, and illegal narcotics totally. These pose major threats to your baby's growth. Be cautious with certain drugs and herbal supplements, always visiting your doctor before taking anything new.

Safe environment: Avoid exposure to dangerous chemicals, poisons, and secondhand smoke. Ensure your house and workplace are safe from potential threats.

Emotional well-being: Pregnancy can be an emotional rollercoaster. Acknowledge your sensations, allow yourself to experience joy, worry, or even terror. Talk to loved ones, join support groups, or seek professional counseling if needed. Remember, you are not alone on this path.

Additional Tips:
Build a solid support system: Surround yourself with caring and supportive relatives and friends who can offer emotional and practical help.

Stay informed: Seek credible sources of information on pregnancy, labor, and baby care. Attend childbirth education seminars or workshops.

Plan for the future: Discuss childcare choices, budgets, and family leave rules with your partner.

Listen to your body: Every pregnancy is unique. Pay attention to how you feel, follow your intuition, and communicate honestly with your healthcare professional.

Remember:
This information is for general knowledge and should not be taken as medical advice. Always consult your healthcare practitioner for tailored advice and address any unique concerns you might have.

Don't hesitate to ask questions, voice your concerns, and actively participate in your prenatal care.

Embrace the journey, appreciate the milestones, and nurture both your physical and emotional well-being to create a healthy and pleasant pregnant experience.

Building on the core facts you currently have, let's go deeper into prenatal care and healthy practices with even more details:

Prenatal Care:
First Trimester:
Early dating ultrasound: Confirms pregnancy, estimates due date, and checks for multiple babies.

Blood tests: Screen for anemia, immunity to certain diseases, hereditary risks, and blood type.

Initial discussion: Explore your medical history, family history, lifestyle choices, and birth preferences.

Second Trimester:
Anatomy scan ultrasound: Evaluates your baby's organs and development for abnormalities.

Maternal serum alpha-fetoprotein (MSAFP) and quad screen: Identify potential risks for Down syndrome and other chromosomal abnormalities.

Glucose tolerance test: Screens for gestational diabetes.

Third Trimester:
Non-stress test (NST) and/or biophysical profile (BPP): Assess fetal well-being through movement, heart rate, and breathing activity.

Group B strep test: Screens for a bacterial infection that can be transferred to your kid at delivery.

Discussions: Refine birth plans, explore pain management options, and prepare for delivery and newborn care.

Healthy Habits:

Diet:
Specific nutrients: Emphasize folic acid (400 mcg daily), iron (27 mg daily), calcium (1000mg daily), and vitamin D (600 IU daily).

Foods to limit: Processed meats, sugary drinks, raw or undercooked fish, unpasteurized dairy products, and excessive caffeine.

Sample meal plan:

Breakfast: Greek yogurt with berries and granola, whole-wheat toast with avocado, or oatmeal with nuts and seeds.

Lunch: Salad with grilled chicken or fish, whole-wheat sandwich with lean protein and veggies, or lentil soup with whole-grain bread.

Dinner: Salmon with roasted vegetables, quinoa bowl with black beans and roasted veggies, or chicken stir-fry with brown rice.

Snacks: Fruits, veggies with hummus, yogurt with fruit, whole-wheat crackers with cheese, or air-popped popcorn.

Exercise: Specific activities: Walking, swimming, prenatal yoga, Pilates, dancing, low-impact aerobics, and strength training suitable for pregnancy.

Modifications: Listen to your body, abbreviate sessions as needed, and avoid workouts that raise your risk of falling or abdominal strain.

Warm-up and cool-down: Essential to prevent injury.

Sleep: Relaxation techniques: Deep breathing, progressive muscular relaxation, meditation, and mindfulness activities.

Create a sleep-conducive environment: Cool temperature, darkness, stillness, and comfy bedding.

Avoid screen time before bed: The blue light emitted can interfere with sleep.

Stress management:
Journaling: Write down your ideas and feelings to digest them properly.

Spending time in nature: Walking in parks, gardening, or sitting by a window can be peaceful.

Connecting with loved ones: Talk to friends, relatives, or a therapist for support and shared experiences.

Mindfulness techniques: Focus on the present moment and let go of stress and rumination.

Additional Tips:
Dental care: Regular dental examinations and adequate oral hygiene are vital throughout pregnancy.

Skincare: Use soft, fragrance-free products and moisturize daily, especially as your belly develops.

Travel: Consult your doctor before going, especially internationally, regarding immunizations and any hazards.

Legal rights and resources: Explore your rights as a pregnant and postpartum person, and familiarize yourself with relevant resources like maternity leave policies and government support programs.

Remember:
Individualized care: This information is a general guide. Consult your healthcare professional for individualized advice based on your specific needs and health history.

Open communication: Don't hesitate to ask questions, voice your concerns, and actively engage in your healthcare decisions.

Support system: Surround yourself with loving and supportive individuals who can offer emotional and practical help.

Embrace the journey: Celebrate the milestones, listen to your body, and trust your instincts as you create a healthy and pleasant pregnancy experience.

I hope this complete guide enables you to make informed choices, prioritize your health and feel confident as you embark on this beautiful road to motherhood!

Conclusion

Unveiling the Gift of Parenthood

As you close this book, I hope you feel empowered with information and renewed confidence on your journey to parenting. Remember, this path is unique for everyone, and there's no one-size-fits-all strategy. Embrace the exploration, appreciate the minor triumphs, and most importantly, be nice to yourself and your spouse throughout the process.

Key Takeaways:

Your body is amazing: You've learned about the complicated ballet of hormones, the fertile window, and the miracle process of conception. Remember, your body is intrinsically geared for procreation, and mastering its rhythms is your superpower.

Knowledge is power: This book has provided you with useful tools and insights. Utilize the fertility charting methods, examine the natural ways, and make educated decisions connected with your personal beliefs and preferences.

Communication is key: Open and honest communication with your partner is crucial. Share your hopes, worries, and discoveries. Celebrate one other's efforts and support each other through the ups and downs.

Enjoy the journey: Don't let the quest of pregnancy overshadow the pleasure of intimacy and connection. Embrace the shared experience, find delight in the act of making love, and realize that even if conception takes longer than intended, the trip itself is a gift.

Looking Forward:

Continue learning: As your understanding of your body and fertility evolves, stay curious and keep exploring. There are innumerable tools available to improve your knowledge and provide continuing help.

Seek help: If you have worries or encounter obstacles, don't hesitate to seek expert guidance from a healthcare physician or fertility specialist. They can offer individualized guidance and support targeted to your unique situation.

Embrace the unknown: Remember, conception is a lovely mystery, and occasionally things don't go according to plan. Embrace the unexpected, be cheerful, and trust that whatever route unfolds will lead you where you're intended to be.

May this book be a stepping stone on your route to fatherhood. Remember, you are not alone in this. With education, love, and steadfast hope, you are well on your way to unlocking the marvel of life.

Cracking the Fertile Code: A Legacy of Love and Laughter

As you reach the final page, don't let the journey finish here. Remember, "Cracking the Fertile Code" wasn't just about attaining pregnancy; it was about empowering you to build a legacy of love and joy.

Imagine:

The small fingers curled around yours, the gummy smiles that melt your heart, the echoes of laughing filling your home.

The shared stories of "remember when we were trying?" spoken with fondness and mirth.

The unshakable love that emerges from shared trials and successes, a love fostered from the very beginning of your family's journey.

Let this book be a reminder to:

Cherish the process: The suspense, the exhilaration, the nervous laughter - they are all threads sewn into the tapestry of your love tale. Embrace them, for they make the arrival of your little miracle all the more lovely.

Celebrate every milestone: From the first positive test to the first kick, each step deserves a moment of excitement. Share these successes with loved ones, creating memories that will long link you together.

Nurture your relationship: Parenthood is an adventure, but it can also challenge the strongest connections. Prioritize quality time with your partner, keep the spark alive, and remember that you are a team on this beautiful journey.

Remember:

Every family is unique, and your path will be too. Embrace the unexpected twists and turns, for they often lead to the most beautiful places.

There will be moments of doubt and frustration, but never lose sight of the love that brought you here. Draw strength from each other, and allow your love to be your guiding light.

Above all, have fun! Laughter is the finest medicine, and a joyous heart produces a caring environment for your expanding family.

So, conclude this book with a grin, knowing that you are not simply armed with knowledge, but also empowered to build a legacy of love, laughter, and unlimited possibilities. May your road to parenting be filled with amazement, love, and the joyful echo of tiny giggles that will forever be the sweetest music to your ears.

Cracking the Fertile Code: A Blend of Hope and Inspiration

As you conclude this book, you might feel a combination of feelings - exhilaration, hope, maybe even a hint of uncertainty. Remember, you're not alone. Every successful pregnancy began with a first step, a seed of hope planted within the heart.

This book wasn't only about cracking the fruitful code. It was about empowering you to begin on a magnificent path of self-discovery, understanding your body, and nurturing the fertile ground of your dreams.

Think of this book as a single thread, weaved into the bigger tapestry of your life. As you move on, remember to:

Embrace the Unexpected: Don't be disheartened if your path takes a different turn than intended. Detours often lead to hidden gems, and sometimes the most beautiful stories unfold in the most unexpected ways.

Share Your Story: Your experience, challenges, and successes can inspire others on their own journey. Share your story, whether it's whispered to a confidante, written in a notebook, or shared on an internet forum. You never know who you might touch with your courage and vulnerability.

Pay it Forward: As you manage motherhood, remember the help you got along the way. Offer a helping hand to others on their road, offering your wisdom and compassion.

Finally, remember that Cracking the Fertile Code is not the conclusion of your narrative, but the beginning of a new chapter, full of love, laughter, and the astounding miracle of life.

May your path be blessed with:

Patience and Grace: As you negotiate the ups and downs, treat yourself and your body with kindness. Remember, even nature works in cycles, and sometimes the wait is simply part of the magic.

Unwavering Hope: Never lose sight of the dream that brought you here. Hold onto that hope, let it drive your resilience, and know that with patience and perseverance, your dreams will emerge.

Everlasting Love: Cherish the love that brought you together and produced this family. Nurture it through thick and thin, for it will be the cornerstone of your greatest adventure yet.

So, conclude this book with a heart full of hope, an open mind eager for adventure, and a soul brimming with love. Remember, the story you're writing is unique, powerful, and packed with unlimited possibilities. Go forth, make your legacy, and never forget the magic that started it all - Cracking the Fertile Code.

Congratulations on going on this great trip!

Congratulations, and best wishes for a lifetime of love and fun!

Congratulations, and may your journey be blessed with the echoes of laughter and the whispers of love.